The Blue Max Airmen

German Airmen Awarded the Pour le Mérite

Volume 5

Manfred von Richthofen

Lance J. Bronnenkant, PhD.

The Blue Max Airmen
German Airmen Awarded the Pour le Mérite
Volume 5
Manfred von Richthofen
Lance J. Bronnenkant, PhD.

I would like to thank the following colleagues who generously contributed to this work: Thomas Genth, Jack Herris, Jim Miller, Terry Phillips, and Greg VanWyngarden.

Interested in WWI aviation? Join The League of WWI Aviation Historians (**www.overthefront.com**) and Cross & Cockade International (**www.crossandcockade.com**)

Design and layout: Jack Herris
Cover design: Aaron Weaver
Aircraft Colors and Markings: Greg VanWyngarden
Color Profiles: Jim Miller
Digital photo editing: Aaron Weaver & Jack Herris

Publisher's Cataloging-in-Publication data

Bronnenkant, Lance J.
    The Blue Max Airmen: German Aviators Awarded the Pour le Mérite: Volume 5 / by Lance J. Bronnenkant.
    p. cm.
    ISBN 978-1-935881-29-2
1. Richthofen, Mandred 1892–1918. 2. World War, 1914–1918 --Aerial operations, German. 3. Fighter pilots -- Germany. 4. Aeronautics, Military --Germany -- History. II. Title.

ND237 .S6322 2011
759.13 --dc22
                           2011904920

Aeronaut Books

www.aeronautbooks.com

Table of Contents

Manfred von Richthofen
  The Man   6
  The Aircraft   52
  Military Service   116
  Victory List   118
Color Profile Commentaries (Greg VanWyngarden)   122
Pour le Mérite Winners by Date of Award   128
Pour le Mérite Winners Alphabetically   129
Index   130
Bibliography   133
Glossary   134
Errata & Addenda   135

Right: A rare color print of the upper portion of Fritz Reusing's 1917 painting of Manfred von Richthofen (see page 12).

Rittmeister Manfred Frhr. von Richthofen

Above: A replication, using authentic period decorations, of Manfred von Richthofen's *Ordenskissen* as displayed at the Richthofen Museum in Schweidnitz. Top row (left to right): Iron Cross, 1st Class (Prussia); Pilot's Badge, Army (Germany); Red Eagle Order, 3rd Class with Crown and Swords (Prussia); *Pour le Mérite* (Prussia); Field Pilot's Badge, Army (Austria-Hungary); War Medal (Ottoman Empire). Middle row: War Honor Cross for Heroic Act (Lippe); *Feldschnalle* (ribbons bar); Imtiaz Medal in Silver (Ottoman Empire); Liakat Medal in Silver (Ottoman Empire). Bottom row: Bravery Order, 4th Class, 1st Degree (Bulgaria); *Grossordenschnalle* (medals bar) displaying Iron Cross, 2nd Class (Prussia); Royal Hohenzollern House Order, Knight's Cross with Swords (Prussia); Military St. Henry Order, Knight's Cross (Saxony); Saxe-Ernestine House Order, Knight 1st Class with Swords (Saxon Duchies); Military Merit Order, 4th Class with Crown and Swords (Bavaria); Military Merit Order, Knight (Württemberg); Oval Silver Duke Carl Eduard Medal with Date Clasp and Swords (Saxe-Goburg-Gotha); General Honor Decoration "For Bravery" (Hesse); Cross for Faithful Service, 2nd Class (Schaumburg-Lippe); War Merit Cross, 2nd Class (Brunswick); Hanseatic Cross (Lübeck); Hanseatic Cross (Bremen); Hanseatic Cross (Hamburg); Order of the Iron Crown, 3rd Class with War Decoration (Austria-Hungary); Military Merit Cross, 3rd Class with War Decoration (Austria-Hungary).

Facing Page: A portrait of Manfred von Richthofen that was taken at C.J. von Dühren's studio in Berlin during Richthofen's brief time there on 2–3 February 1916 on his way home to Schweidnitz. He had just been awarded his *Pour le Mérite* on 12 January. This iconic image was published as card no.503 in Willi Sanke's famous postcard series.

Manfred von Richthofen

Rittmeister Freiherr v. Richthofen
+ 21. 4. 1918

v. Dühren & Henschel phot.
Berlin

Left & Above: Two versions of a smiling portrait of Manfred von Richthofen that was taken the same time as the one displayed on Sanke card 503 (see page 4). The one above was personally dedicated by Richthofen, while the one at left was a postcard produced by *"den Freunden und Förderern der Deutschen Luftfahrt"* ("the Friends and Supporters of German Aviation") to commemorate his death.

Manfred von Richthofen – The Man

Manfred von Richthofen, also widely known as "The Red Baron" thanks to Peanuts cartoon strip creator Charles M. Schulz, is unquestionably the most famous figure to emerge from World War I aviation.[1] Numerous books and articles have been devoted to almost every aspect of his life and career, with Peter Kilduff's *Richthofen: Beyond the Legend of the Red Baron* and *The Illustrated Red Baron*, along with Jim Miller's *Manfred von Richthofen: The Aircraft, Myths and Accomplishments of 'The Red Baron,'* being the most recent, comprehensive, and reliable studies. So what follows is largely a synopsis of the decades of work performed to date by a whole host of researchers. Readers are advised to turn to sources such as those above to delve more

deeply into the life of Manfred von Richthofen.

Youth and Early Career

On Monday, 2 May 1892, Manfred Albrecht von Richthofen was born to Major Albrecht Philipp Karl Julius von Richthofen and his wife, Kunigunde Hildegard Marie Luise Elisabeth (née von Schickfus und Neudorff), in Breslau (now Wrocław, Poland). He was their second child but first son, having been preceded by his sister Elisabeth ("Ilse") Therese Elfriede two years earlier in 1890. The couple's third child, Lothar Siegfried, followed in 1894; and their fourth, Karl Bolko Alexander, was born in 1903

Right: A servant looks after Ilse von Richthofen and her younger brother Manfred as he drives a goat-drawn cart around family property.

after the family had moved to Schweidnitz (now Švidnica, Poland). By all accounts, Manfred enjoyed his childhood, excelling in swimming, gymnastics, and other athletic pursuits. His greatest love, however, was hunting, which he learned to do at an early age though somewhat inauspiciously. His mother recalled during an interview with author Floyd Gibbons:

"We passed our vacations in the country with Grandmother. One day, Manfred could not suppress his fast-developing passion for hunting. He had his first air rifle, and with it he killed three or four of Grandmother's tame ducks that he found swimming on a little pond near the house. He proudly related his exploit to his grandmother, and I started to reprimand him. His good old grandmother stopped me from scolding him because, as she said, he had been right in confessing his misdeed. Today, when I see those three duck feathers in his old room with all his trophies of war, I cannot keep back my tears."[2]

Manfred entered the military at an early age. In August 1903, when he was just 11 years old, he was enrolled in the Cadet Academy at Wahlstatt (now Legnickie Pole, Poland). As he himself observed: "I was not particularly eager to become a cadet, but my father wished it, and I was not consulted."[3] He disliked the "strict discipline and order" he found there and by his own admission did just enough school work to barely get by.[4] His situation improved in 1909 when he graduated to the Senior Cadet Academy at Gross-Lichterfelde at age 17. He commented:

"I liked it much better at Lichterfelde. I did not feel so isolated from the world and I began to live more like a human being."[5]

Part of his training involved horse riding and he developed a deep passion for it, participating in several competitions. By 1911, he had decided to enter the cavalry and was accepted as a *Fahnenjunker* (officer candidate) by *Ulanen-Regiment Kaiser Alexander III. von Russland (Westpreussisches) Nr.1*, based in Militsch (now Milicz, Poland) with a garrison outpost a little further east at Ostrowo (now Ostrów Wielkopolski). He underwent advanced officer training at the *Kriegsschule* (War School) in Berlin the same year and received his officer's patent on 19 November 1912. During his pre-war years, Richthofen struck up a friendship with fellow *Kaiser Alexander III. von Russland Leutnant* Alfred Gerstenberg (officer's patent 18 August 1913), who would later serve in many of the same aviation units as he did.

Early War Years

Richthofen began the war with a patrol from Ostrowo into Russian Poland. He and his small troop barely escaped with their lives when a larger Russian force entered the town in which they had quartered themselves. A short time later he and his men were transported to the Western Front to a position northeast of Diedenhofen, where they disembarked and marched through Luxembourg into Belgium near Arlon. Once again, Richthofen escaped any harm when a superior force of French dragoons surprised his troop of 15. Many of his men were not as lucky as he was, however, and less than half survived the encounter.

This brings us to an account in *Der rote*

Above: Manfred (in cadet uniform) and brother Lothar oversee their youngest sibling, Bolko, as he rides on a sled pulled by the family dog.

Kampfflieger that some believe sheds a dark shadow on Richthofen's legacy. He mentioned being on patrol during the Battle of Virton, which occurred in late August 1914. He and his men stopped at a Belgian monastery that had large stables that could accommodate their horses:

"The monks were extremely amiable. They gave us as much as we wanted to eat and drink and we enjoyed it very much... In other words, we settled down as if we were on maneuvers with a dear host in the evening. Incidentally, several of the hosts hung from a lamp post three days afterwards because they had been unable to resist participating in the war. But on this evening, they were extremely amiable."[6]

It is generally conceded that German troops committed various atrocities against neutral Belgian citizens at this time (hangings, executions, etc.) under the flimsy excuse that they had been aiding and abetting the enemy. Some modern historians have pointed to the passage above as indicating that Richthofen participated in those atrocities. This controversy was unfortunately fueled by some translators choosing to interpret *"hingen"* ("hung") as *"(wir) hingen"* ("(we) hanged") in several works.[7] This was an error, however, because passages that

followed make it clear that Richthofen and his troop moved on and returned to their regiment the next day:

"The next morning the sun was high up in the sky when we woke up from our refreshing sleep. After a good breakfast we continued our journey... We came through the village of Robelmont, which we had seen our infantry occupy on the previous day... In late afternoon I reached my regiment and was quite satisfied with the outcome of the last twenty-four hours."[8]

Thus there is no indication that Richthofen returned to the monastery a few days later and directly participated in the hangings. Even when we accept this (some still do not), it has also been pointed out that the casual and almost flippant way that Richthofen referred to their executions was at the very least a reflection of his callous support of such actions. This may very well be true. It has also been counterargued that he may have believed a report that they had been collaborators who had led to the death or injury of some of his comrades in arms. Others even feel that the passage may have been inserted or altered by Richthofen's ghost writer – but all of this falls in the realm of speculation.[9]

Right: Richthofen's passion for hunting is well known. Here he poses with the elk (called a moose in North America) he shot at the Neu-Sternberg game preserve on 29 September 1917 while on an enforced leave from the front. The father of *Jasta* 11's Eberhardt Mohnicke was the Forest Master there.

With no other facts to rely upon, we are each left to our own opinions on the true significance of this controversial passage.

Richthofen reveled in his cavalry role as the "eyes" of the army, and aviation was far from his thoughts in the early months of the war. In fact, he initially viewed aviators with a certain amount of disdain:

"I had no idea what our fliers did at the time. At any rate, I considered each flier to be an enormous fraud. I couldn't tell who was a German and who was the enemy."[10]

But Richthofen soon found himself bogged down in the trench warfare around Verdun: "I was degraded from being one of the fighting men to being a rear echelon swine."[11] His frustration was abundantly evident in a 2 November 1914 letter he wrote from Béchamps:

"The positions before Verdun haven't shifted 50 meters in weeks. We are located in a burned-out village. Wedel and I live in a house in which you have to hold your nose. We seldom if ever ride... in other words, there's no movement at all. Pretty much everything is making me gain weight – so I'm now as round as a barrel...I so much would like to have earned the Iron Cross 1st Class, but have had no opportunity to do so. So I'll have to disguise myself as a Frenchman and run to Verdun and blow a gun turret sky high."[12]

In early 1915, while serving as an ordnance officer with the 18th Infantry Brigade, Richthofen changed his opinion about aviators and applied to the *Fliegertruppe* (Air Service) for observer training. At that time, the observer was usually the senior

member of the crew in charge of any flight. He was accepted and stopped home on 21 May on his way to his new assignment. His mother recalled:

"Then Manfred, stopping in front of me, unexpectedly said: 'I'm going to [join] the fliers.' There was something beautiful and happy in his voice as he said it; I understood nothing and could imagine little about it... I just listened full of interest to what he had to say about his new [service] arm. When we stepped back into the house from the garden, I felt certain that a new and great mission had taken root in him. Manfred left again four days later."[13]

Observer

Richthofen arrived at *Flieger-Ersatz-Abteilung* 7's base near Cologne as one of thirty candidates sent there for observer evaluation. His first flight occurred the next morning and the thrill of flying soon left his "miserable" start behind:

"The propeller blast bothered me tremendously. Communicating with the pilot was impossible for me. Everything flew away from me. I took out a piece of paper and it disappeared. My crash helmet slipped, my scarf loosened, my jacket was not buttoned up tight enough – in short, it was miserable. Before I knew what was happening, we began to tear off, the pilot gave it full throttle, and the machine began to roll faster and faster. I hung on desperately. All of a sudden, the shuddering stopped and the machine was in the air. The ground rushed out from under me. I had been told where I was to fly, or rather where I was to have directed my pilot to. We flew straight ahead for awhile, then my pilot

Above: A snapshot of a casually dressed Richthofen (far left) at *B.A.O.* while his finger was healing from his 4 September 1915 accident. After Richthofen (left to right): *Freiherr* von Könitz, *Lt.* Hans Haller von Hallerstein, unknown.

turned, turned again, to the right, to the left, and I lost all orientation to my own airfield. I no longer had any idea where I was! I very cautiously began to look at what was below me. The tiny little people, the houses like something from children's building sets, everything so cute and dainty. Cologne lay in the background – the Cologne Cathedral a plaything. It was a sublime feeling, floating over everything. Who could touch me now? No one! I couldn't have cared less that I didn't know where I was, and I was quite sad when my pilot said that it was time to land."[14]

Richthofen's utter failure to carry out his assigned task must have been viewed as subordinate to his enthusiasm and comfort with flying because he was one of the final candidates chosen for further training. He was sent to *FEA* 6 at Grossenhain on 10 June, and then after only a week or so, assigned to *Feldflieger-Abteilung* 69 on the Eastern Front to complete his three-month course:

"Through June, July, and August 1915, I stayed with the *Flieger-Abteilung*, which participated in Mackensen's entire advance from Gorlice to Brest-Litovsk. I had arrived there as a really green observer and didn't have a clue about what I was doing. As a cavalryman, my job had been reconnaissance, so the current service was in my line and I thoroughly enjoyed the long reconnaissance flights we took almost daily."[15]

Richthofen flew first with *Lt.* Georg Zeumer. After Zeumer was transferred to *Brieftauben-Abteilung Ostende*, he drew Count Erich von Holck as his pilot. Toward the end of their partnership, Richthofen and Holck were brought down in disputed territory but managed to link up with German troops in the area and make it back to their outfit. Then on 21 August 1915:

"...I was suddenly transferred to a *Grosskampfflugzeug* [large combat plane] at *B.A.O.* Ostend. There I met an old acquaintance, Zeumer, and the name 'large combat plane' captivated me as well."[16]

Brieftauben-Abteilung Ostende had been established in November 1914 as Germany's first bombing unit under the direct control of Supreme Headquarters (as opposed to a local Army command). Though it employed single-seat monoplanes and regular biplanes as well, the larger

Above: After serving together at *B.A.O.*, Richthofen and Paul Henning von Osterroht would cross paths again as *Jasta* COs. Here is one of several photos taken of the two men (Osterroht was by then a *Hauptmann*) when *Jasta* 11 joined *Jasta* 12 at its Epinoy airfield to discuss a joint operation planned for 15 April 1917. Their discussion is taking place on the wing of *Jasta* 11's D.III 2006/16. Osterroht was killed in action roughly one week later on 23 April.

Grosskampfflugzeuge such as the AEG G.II were at its very heart. The AEG G.II was well armed with either two or three machine guns, and as Richthofen observed: "The name alone [i.e., "large combat plane"] gave us such great courage that we felt no opponent would be able to escape us."[17] Following their first air-to-air fight in it on 1 September, however, their confidence must have waned because an English plane was able to get on their tail and empty its guns into them. Richthofen's opinion of the type was hardly enhanced by a 4 September incident in which, while attempting to point out to Zeumer where one of their bombs had hit, the tip of the little finger on his outstretched right hand was smacked by one of the plane's rotating propellers. This was not how Richthofen had envisioned shedding his first "drop of blood for the Fatherland."[18] So as he put it, they "...soon realized that though the thing was indeed a 'large' plane, it would never make a 'combat' plane."[19]

Richthofen occasionally flew as an observer in the unit's smaller biplanes, and it was on one such occasion that he and his pilot, *Oblt.* Paul Henning von Osterroht, attacked a French Farman. Richthofen recounted:

"Osterroht skilfully flew up so close to him that I was able to bring him well under fire...after I had shot 100 rounds from my cartridge box, I could scarcely believe my eyes as the opponent suddenly went down in very peculiar spirals. I followed him with my eyes and patted Osterroht on the head. He kept falling and falling and actually fell in a large shell hole; you could see him standing on his head there, tail in the air. I definitely located it on the map: he lay five kilometers behind the current lines. So we had shot him down on the other side. At that time, however, kills across the lines were not counted, otherwise I would have one more on my list now."[20]

B.A.O. was redeployed from Gistel to Rethel on

Left: This presumably was the painting of Richthofen done by Fritz Reusing that was displayed in Schulte's Art Gallery in Berlin. (see pages 3, 38–39.)

1 October to help bolster the German air presence in the region during the Second Battle of the Champagne. *Brieftauben-Abteilung Metz, B.A.O.*'s sister unit, loaned them four machines and their crews in support. Among the *B.A.M.* contingent was fighter pilot *Lt.* Oswald Boelcke, and it was on the train trip from Gistel to Rethel that Richthofen first met the man who would become his mentor and idol:

"The Battle of the Champagne was raging. The French airmen were attracting attention. We were assembled into a fighting squadron and went there on 1 October 1915. A young, unpretentious 2nd lieutenant sat at the next table in the dining car. There was no particular reason for him to attract any attention except for one outstanding fact: he was the only one of us who had already shot down an enemy flier – and not just one, but four. He'd even been mentioned by name in the Army Reports. He impressed me because of his quite dashing experiences. Despite my great efforts, I had nothing to show for them, that is, nothing that had been officially acknowledged. So I wanted to learn how this 2Lt. Boelcke really did it. So I engaged him and asked: 'Tell me honestly, how do you really do it?' He laughed, quite amused, even though I had posed the question in all seriousness. Then he answered me: 'Well, good heavens, it's really quite simple. I fly right up to him, aim well, and then he just falls down.' I just shook my head and thought that I'd done that too, only they hadn't fallen down for me. The difference was, however, that he flew a Fokker and I my big combat plane.

I made an effort to get to know this nice, unassuming man, who had made such an impression on me. We often played cards together, went for walks, and I asked him many questions. Thus I gradually came to the conclusion: 'You must learn to fly a Fokker yourself, then things will go much better.'"[21]

Pilot

Richthofen was true to his word. He immediately talked Zeumer into giving him flying lessons; and just a short time later, on 10 October 1915, Zeumer pronounced Richthofen ready for his first solo attempt:

"He explained each theoretical control movement to me once again: I only partially listened because I was firmly convinced: you'll forget half of it. I rolled to the takeoff spot, gave it gas, the machine reached its designated speed, and then I suddenly couldn't help but notice that I was actually flying. Eventually, I felt daring instead of anxious. I didn't have a care in the world. No matter what happened, I wouldn't be frightened again. Contemptuous of death, I made a wide turn to the left, switched off the gas precisely over the designated tree, and waited to see what would happen next. Now came the most difficult part, the landing. I remembered the essential control movements. I performed them mechanically, but the machine reacted differently than usual when Zeumer sat there. I was thrown off balance, made some wrong movements, stood the plane on its head, and there it was: just another 'school machine.'[22] I looked at the damage (which fortunately turned out to be quickly remedied) quite sadly amid ridicule from all sides."[23]

Two weeks after this embarrassing solo result, Richthofen took the first of three pilot examinations required to earn the Pilot's Badge. He failed. Not one to be easily discouraged, he decided he would have to undergo formal pilot training at an established military flight center and applied for the course at Döberitz outside of Berlin. While awaiting word, he was told that he would be flying in one of Germany's *Riesenflugzeuge*, or giant airplanes, in the future. He and his pilot, Osterroht, went to Berlin in order to become familiar with the new type, and Richthofen fortuitously found himself in the vicinity when his assignment to *FEA* 2 at Döberitz came through on 15 November 1915. Within a matter of weeks, Richthofen passed his first two pilot examinations. The third and final test required a cross-country flight and Richthofen chose to satisfy that and his own interest in fighter aircraft by flying to the Fokker factory at Schwerin-Görries – but not before

coming home to celebrate Christmas Eve with his family. His mother recalled happily:

"Fate has been kind to us. Our wishes have been fulfilled. We celebrated Christmas together and you could almost feel yourself transported back to earlier, carefree times. Once again, I stood with my four children under the Christmas tree. I sat down at the piano and played 'Silent Night, Holy Night.' Manfred and Ilse sang along splendidly with their beautiful, clear voices. Lothar (utterly tone deaf and without a singing voice) kept his mouth shut, but his eyes shone all the brighter. All three, and Bolko too, were in uniform; Ilse in her nurse's outfit."[24]

Richthofen returned to Berlin on Christmas Day and made his roundtrip flight to Schwerin-Görries from there. Then, perhaps using the examination requirement as a convenient excuse, he made another long trip: Berlin—Breslau—Schweidnitz—Lüben—Berlin. This of course afforded him a further opportunity to visit relatives and family during the Christmas season.

Richthofen gained more flight experience with *FEA* 2 before he was assigned as a pilot to *Kampfgeschwader der Obersten Heeresleitung Nr.2* (Supreme Command's Combat Squadron No.2). Known as *Kagohl* 2 in its abbreviated form, it had been created from the former *Brieftauben-Abteilung Metz* on 20 December 1915 and reorganized into six *Kampstaffeln* or *Kastas* (combat units). Richthofen reported to one of them, *Kasta* 8, at Mont near the Verdun front on 16 March 1916 and began to fly two-seaters. He made his second victory claim (his first as a pilot, though) and earned his first mention in the *Heeresbericht* (Army Report) dated 26 April 1916. A little earlier, he had had a machine gun mounted to fire forward under his control above his plane's propeller arc:

"One could well laugh at it a little because it looked quite primitive. But I swore by it, of course, and soon had the opportunity to put it to practical use. I encountered a Nieuport, [whose pilot] apparently was a beginner too, because he behaved awfully foolishly. I flew toward him, whereupon he ran away. Evidently, he had suffered a gun jam. I didn't get the feeling that I would be able to engage him in battle: 'What would happen though if you shot at him?' I flew at him and for the first time, at a very, very close distance, pressed the machine gun button; there was a short series of shots and my Nieuport reared up and flipped over. At first my observer and I thought it was one of the many tricks that some of the Frenchmen are accustomed to pulling. This trick, however, didn't end and it went deeper and deeper; then my 'Franz' patted me on the head and yelled out: 'Congratulations, he's falling!'

Above: Richthofen chats with his *Kasta* 8 CO, *Hptm*. Viktor Carganico.

In fact, he fell into a forest behind Fort Douamount and disappeared among the trees. It was clear to me: 'You've shot that one down.' However – on the other side of the lines!"[25]

The 26 April 1916 *Heeresbericht* read: "Two enemy aircraft were shot down in air combat over Fleury, south of Douaumont and west thereof." Nevertheless, Richthofen received no official credit for the victory. The *Heeresbericht* normally related the prior days' events, which meant that Richthofen's action had probably taken place on 25 April. *Sous-Lt.* Mathieu Tenant de La Tour, a Nieuport pilot from *Escadrille* N57 which was based north of Lemmes along the Verdun Road, was reported as wounded in action that day and may have been Richthofen's quarry.

Richthofen's elation was dampened by the death of his former *B.A.O.* pilot, Count Erich von Holck, on 30 April at the hands of future French ace *Lt.* Albert Deullin of *Escadrille* N3. Holck, at this point an *Eindecker* fighter pilot with *KEK* Jametz, had been shot through the head during a fight that Richthofen witnessed from the air: "It affected me deeply, because he was not only a model of courage but also a man of rare personality."[26] Richthofen had visited Holck just three days earlier, no doubt to celebrate the former's first (though unconfirmed) victory as a pilot.

Fighter Pilot

On 3 May 1916, the day of Erich von Holck's funeral, Richthofen told his parents about his new role at *Kagohl* 2:

"In the morning, I had three very exhilarating air combats, and in the evening I was sitting with Zeumer, my first pilot, with a punch bowl under a blossoming apple tree until one in the morning. I feel quite well in my new occupation as a combat aviator (pilot); I think no other post in this war would be able to attract me more than this one. I am flying a Fokker, which is the airplane with which Boelcke and Immelmann have been tremendously successful."[27]

Shortly after his arrival at *Kagohl* 2, Richthofen had pestered his CO, *Hptm.* Viktor Carganico, to allow him to go to the *Armee-Flug-Park* at Montmédy for single-seat fighter training.[28] Carganico eventually agreed, and after Richthofen's return, allowed him and *Lt.* Hans Reimann to share an *Eindecker* – Richthofen flying it in the morning and Reimann in the afternoon. Their partnership ended a few weeks later, however, after Reimann was brought down in no-man's-land and had to set fire to the plane to prevent its capture. Richthofen was then given a second *Eindecker* to fly, but after only a few flights crashed it in late June during an emergency landing caused by engine failure. Carganico subsequently gave Richthofen permission to fly his personal machine. But the fledging fighter pilot sought more action and experience:

"I'm thinking about going to Boelcke to become his student. I'm always in need of change. That would be something new again and not to my detriment."[29]

Fate may have seemed cruel to Richthofen, however, when *Kagohl* 2 was suddenly transferred to the Eastern Front on 28 June and Boelcke was sent off on leave. Whatever plans Richthofen had had to reach out to Boelcke would have to wait. He found himself relegated to piloting C-type aircraft again, usually in bombing runs against Russian forces east of Kowel (now Kovel', Ukraine). He wrote that he enjoyed the immediate results that a bomb drop could bring and that strafing ground forces was a satisfying activity as well. Nevertheless, events in August would prove that he was a fighter pilot at heart.

Boelcke

Oswald Boelcke, a *Hauptmann* since May 1916, was Germany's Ace of Aces with 19 victories when he went on leave at the end of June to tour some of Germany's allied countries including Austria-Hungary, Turkey, and Bulgaria. His was an enforced

Above: According to the inscription on the back of this photograph, it was a group shot of *Kampfgeschwader der Obersten Heeresleitung* 2 airmen at Lesnaja on 26 July 1916. *Geschwaderführer Hptm.* Gustav Kastner-Kirdorf (2) stands at center, with *Hptm.* Wilhelm Boelcke (1) to the left and *Lt.* Erwin Böhme (3), Richthofen (4), and *Lt.* Alfred Gerstenberg (5) to the right.

leave due to High Command's fear for his safety following the death of Max Immelmann on 18 June, but at least the destinations were of his choosing. Toward the end of his tour, Oswald decided to visit his older brother, Wilhelm, who was the CO of *Kagohl* 2's *Kasta* 10. Arrangements were hastily made and he arrived at Kowel on the morning of 12 August. Awaiting him there was a telegram from *Feldflugchef* Hermann Thomsen that ordered him to return to the Western Front to organize and command one of the new fighter units, *Jagdstaffel* 2. Boelcke asked his brother for input on pilots he thought might be suitable for his new command. Wilhelm mentioned one of his men, 37-year-old *Lt.* Erwin Böhme. *Kasta* 8's *Lt.* Hans Reimann was also brought up. Then there was the man Reimann had shared an *Eindecker* with, Manfred von Richthofen:

"The August sun was almost unbearable at the sandy airfield at Kowel. We comrades were chatting among ourselves, when one said: 'The great Boelcke is coming to visit us, or rather his brother, today in Kowel.' The famous man appeared that evening, we gazed at him in wonder, and he related many interesting things about his trip to Turkey, from where he was just returning to report to Supreme Headquarters. He said that he would be going to the Somme to continue his work there, and would be setting up an entire fighter unit. To that end, he could select the people he deemed appropriate from the Air Service. I dared not ask him to take me with him... Boelcke was due to leave the next morning. Early in the morning there was a sudden knock on my door, and the great man with the *Pour le Mérite*

stood before me. I didn't quite know what he wanted of me. Sure I knew him, as I've already mentioned, but the thought never occurred to me that he had called on me to invite me to be his student. I almost hugged him when he asked me if I wanted to go with him to the Somme.

Three days later, I sat on a train and rode across Germany directly to my new field of activity. At last, my fondest wish was fulfilled, and the most beautiful time of my life was now beginning."[30]

Boelcke's students began assembling at *Jasta* 2's Vélu airfield north of Bertincourt in late August and early September 1916, with Richthofen arriving there on 1 September. At first, they had only a handful of Fokker D-types and one Halberstadt fighter to train with and only one or two pilots could go up with Boelcke at a time. Nevertheless, Boelcke constantly strove to indoctrinate them in the fighter pilot tactics he had developed, and he personally validated them by bringing down no less than seven aircraft in the unit's first two weeks of operation. On 16 September, six new Albatros fighters (five D.Is and a D.II for Boelcke) finally arrived at nearby *AFP* 1 and Boelcke, Richthofen, and others went there to collect them. The following day, for the first time, *Jasta* 2 was able to take to the air in full strength:

"We all stood on the firing range and tried out and adjusted our machine guns, one after the other, as each of us deemed best. Our new apparatuses had come the day before, and Boelcke wanted to fly with us the next morning. We were all beginners; none of us had ever experienced a success. Whatever Boelcke told us was therefore gospel. In recent days, he had,

 Et. Frh.-v. Richthofen

Hpt. Keller

Hptm Boelcke

dahinter gefangene Engländer

Above: Richthofen (back to camera) and *Hptm*. Oswald Boelcke (center) at *AFP* 1, possibly on 16 September 1916 when they went there to collect their Albatros fighters. *AFP* 1's CO, *Hptm*. Alfred Keller, stands between the two men as English prisoners-of-war line up for food in the background. Note that Richthofen is already holding the walking stick that later became known as *JG* 1's *Geschwaderstock*. For another photograph taken on this occasion, see Volume 1 of this series, p.24.

as he put it, shot down at least one and sometimes two Englishmen 'for breakfast.'[31]

The next morning, 17 September, was a wonderful day. We could count on lively activity from the English. Before we went up, Boelcke gave us some precise instructions, and we flew for the first time as a squadron under the command of the famous man to whom we blindly entrusted ourselves.

We had just gotten to the front when we detected, due to shell bursts from our balloon anti-aircraft guns, an enemy squadron over our lines flying in the direction of Cambrai. Naturally, Boelcke was the first to spot them because he saw more than other men. Soon we all grasped the situation too and each strove to stay behind Boelcke. It was clear to us all that we had to pass our first test under the eyes of our revered leader. We approached the squadron slowly because it couldn't escape from us anymore. We were between our opponent and the front. If he wanted to return, he'd have to go by us. We counted the enemy airplanes and definitely determined that there were seven. We were only five, however. All the Englishmen flew large, two-seat bomber planes. Everything was going to break loose in only a matter of seconds. Boelcke was the first to close in on the already damned ones but still didn't shoot. I was the second with my comrades close nearby. The Englishman flying closest to me was a big, darkly-painted barge. I didn't hesitate and got him in my sights. He shot, I shot, I missed, he did too. Then a battle began in which it was important for me, at any rate, to get behind the fellow because I could only fire in my direction of flight. He had no such need because his moveable machine gun could reach all sides. But he appeared to be no beginner, because he knew his final hour would sound the moment I managed to get behind him... So my Englishman twisted and turned, often crossing my line of fire. I gave no thought to other Englishmen from the squadron coming to the aid of their beleaguered comrade. There was only this thought: 'He must fall, come what may!' Then, finally, an opportune moment. The enemy apparently lost sight of me and flew straight ahead. In a split second, I sat on his neck in my good machine. A short burst from my machine gun; I was so close to him that I was afraid I would ram him. Suddenly, I almost cried out aloud with joy because the enemy's propeller stopped spinning. Hurray! He was hit! The motor was shot up and the enemy would have to land on our side because reaching his own lines was out of the question. I also noticed from the apparatus' swaying motion that all wasn't right with the pilot. The observer was not to be seen either; his machine gun stuck up in the air unattended. So I had hit him too and he must have been lying on the floor of the fuselage. The Englishman landed someplace right next to the airfield of a squadron I knew. I was so excited that I couldn't resist touching down and landed at the unfamiliar airfield with such eagerness that I almost stood my machine on its nose. The two airplanes – the Englishmen's and mine – weren't very far apart. I ran there immediately and saw that a number of soldiers were already streaming towards the enemy. Once there, I found that my assumption had been correct. The motor was shot through and both occupants badly injured. The observer died right away and the pilot died during transport to the hospital nearby. In memory of my honorably fallen opponents, I placed a stone on his beautiful grave."[32]

Richthofen then related that when he returned to Vélu, he learned that every member of the flight had achieved a victory as well. *Jasta 2* had waded into a flight of FE.2bs from RFC No.11 Squadron that were flying escort for No.12 Squadron BE.2s on a bombing run against Marcoing. The German group that attacked them actually consisted of six aircraft, as related in Erwin Böhme's more contemporaneous 21 September 1916 letter describing the event (the *Der rote Kampfflieger* passage was dictated eight months later). Six of the English flight's eight planes – four FE.2bs and two BE.2s – were indeed shot down, though only four were officially credited to *Jasta 2*. Boelcke got one and the other three went to Richthofen, Reimann, and Böhme – proof that the Boelcke brothers had chosen wisely back in August at Kowel. Richthofen's unfortunate victims had been 2Lt. Lionel Bertram Frank Morris (pilot) and Lt. Tom Rees (observer) in No.11 Squadron's FE.2b 7018.[33] They both died just as Richthofen had stated – Rees in the air and Morris on the ground soon after their crash. Though Richthofen did not display his victim's cut-out serial number on his wall like he did with so many other of his later victories, air historian James Miller has confirmed that he retained the plane's manufacturing plate, clearly marked with "Boulton & Paul...Machine No.7018."[34]

Jasta 2 never looked back and continued to amass success upon success during its first two months of existence. By the end of October, *Jasta 2* had unequivocally established itself as the *Fliegertruppe's* most accomplished fighter unit. It had achieved 51 official victories since its inception, and its members could boast of the following individual tallies: *Hptm.* Oswald Boelcke – 40, *Oblt.* Stefan Kirmaier – 7, *Lt.* Manfred von Richthofen – 6, *Lt.* Erwin Böhme – 5, *Offz-Stv.* Leopold Reimann – 5, *Lt.* Hans Reimann – 4, *Lt.* Otto Höhne – 3, *Lt.* Hans Imelmann – 3, *Lt.* Winand Grafe – 2, *Offz-Stv.* Max Müller – 2, "patrol" – 1. This was more than double the count of their nearest competitor, *Jasta* 4, that had compiled 24 victories during the same period. Even if we remove Boelcke from the equation, who was responsible for 21 of *Jasta* 2's 51 victories himself, we are still left with a victory total of 30 for the remainder of the unit – again, better than *Jasta* 4 which had *Kanonen* ("big guns" or aces) like Rudolf Berthold, Hans-Joachim Buddecke, Wilhelm Frankl, Walter Höhndorf, and Kurt Wintgens on its roster.

Tragedy struck on 28 October when Oswald Boelcke was killed in the crash landing that ensued after his Albatros D.II collided in midair with *Lt.* Erwin Böhme's D.I. Richthofen witnessed the accident and, like all his comrades and indeed his countrymen, was devastated. He confided in his

Above: A *Kette* of *Jasta* 2 fighter pilots observing something in the sky while resting on *Lt.* Jürgen Sandel's D.I 431/16 at Lagnicourt airfield. Left to right: Sandel, Richthofen (with binoculars), *Lt.* Bodo von Lyncker, *Lt.* Hans Imelmann. This photo was taken after Sandel's, Imelmann's, and Lyncker's arrivals in October but before Lyncker's serious accident on 13 November 1916.

mother: "It had an enormously deep impact on us, as if one of our dearest brothers had been taken."[35] During Boelcke's funeral ceremony in Cambrai, Richthofen was chosen to carry his mentor's *Ordenskissen*, the black cushion upon which his many decorations were displayed. Almost one year later at the end of September 1917, having already surpassed Boelcke to become Germany's Ace of Aces with a tally that then stood at 61 victories, Richthofen's reverance for his former teacher remained abundantly evident when he said to fellow train passenger, Emil August Glogau: "I'm just a combat pilot, but Boelcke, he was a hero."[36] Boelcke's theory and practice of group fighter pilot tactics and training had been amply validated by his students. Now it was up to them to carry his legacy forward; and that is precisely what Manfred von Richthofen did.

Hawker

Richthofen's 80 victories have been intensively studied in multiple publications and will not be detailed here. One that should be mentioned, however, stood out from the rest. It was Richthofen's fight with one of England's leading airmen, Major Lanoe G. Hawker. Hawker, Great Britain's first recipient of the Victoria Cross for air combat, was well known to German airmen who referred to him variously as "the English Boelcke" or "the English Immelmann." On 23 November 1916, a flight of RFC No.24 Squadron DH.2s, led by Hawker, tangled with *Jasta* Boelcke's (following Boelcke's death, the unit was named in his honor) Albatros fighters. Accounts differ as to which man attacked the other first, but all agree that they quickly became engaged in a terrific struggle to see who would get the upper hand.[37] Richthofen recalled:

"The Englishman tried to put himself behind

me while I tried to get behind the Englishman. So we both turned like crazy in circles with motors running flat out at 3,500 meters altitude. First 20 times to the left, then 30 times to the right, each of us intent upon getting above and behind the other. I soon got wise to the fact that I wasn't dealing with a beginner because he never even dreamed of breaking off the fight. He had a very maneuverable crate, but mine climbed better, and so I was able to get above and behind the Englishman. After we had dropped down to 2,000 meters without reaching any result, my opponent must have realized that it was then high time for him to make a push, because the wind was in my favor and had driven us more toward our [German] positions until we had almost arrived at Bapaume, about a kilometer behind our front lines. When we were at 1,000 meters altitude, the cheeky fellow still had the impertinence to cheerily wave at me as if to say: 'Well, well, how do you do?'... Eventually, the brave sportsman had enough of all this and finally had to decide whether he was going to land in our territory or fly back to his own lines. He of course chose the latter after trying in vain to escape me by looping and other such tricks. My first 'blue beans' [i.e, bullets] flew by his ears at that time, because up to then I hadn't fired a shot. At about 100 meters altitude, he tried to escape to the front by flying zigzag, which is known to make it difficult for the observer to shoot well. Now was the moment of truth for me. I followed him from 50 to 30 meters altitude, firing continuously. The Englishman had to fall. A gun jam nearly broke up my success. The opponent, with a shot to the head, crashed about 50 meters behind our lines."[38]

This dogfight has been the subject of many debates during the almost 100 years that have passed since its occurrence, with Hawker's and Richthofen's relative skills and the superiority/inferiority of their respective aircraft at their center. In the final assessment, however, it seems clear that what had essentially been a stalemate was eventually decided by Mother Nature's prevailing wind.

Staffelführer and *Pour le Mérite*
Hawker had counted as Richthofen's 11th victory. Four more followed before the end of 1916, followed by a 16th on 4 January 1917. Richthofen had doubled the total that once qualified pilots for the *Orden Pour le Mérite*, and he was expecting news of its award when a telegram arrive at *Jasta* Boelcke:

"'*Leutnant* v. R. appointed leader of *Jagdstaffel* 11.' I have to say I was annoyed. One was so wonderfully used to working with one's comrades at *Jasta* Boelcke. To have to start all over again with settling in, etc., was for the birds. Besides, I would

have preferred the *Pour le Mérite*."[39]

Two days later, during a *Jasta* Boelcke farewell party for Richthofen, another telegram was delivered that fulfilled Richthofen's wish by informing him that the Kaiser had given him the award he coveted. The award document was dated 12 January 1917 – a year to the day that Oswald Boelcke had gotten his. And so it was that Richthofen arrived at *Jasta* 11's airfield at La Brayelle, outside of Douai, on 22–23 January as Germany's greatest living ace with Prussia's highest award for bravery dangling from his collar.

Richthofen had his work cut out for him: "*Staffel* 11 has been in existence for as long as my old one, only it hasn't shot anyone down yet; so the work here is bringing me very little joy at present."[40] Like his mentor before him, he showed them how it was done during his first days as their leader; but he almost died doing so:

"I was lucky. On my first day [here] I shot no.17 down, on my second day no.18. As I was shooting my 18th down, one of my wings broke in two at 300 meters altitude during the air combat. It was a miracle that I reached the ground without going to pieces."[41]

Richthofen had recently begun using the new Albatros D.III model and had discovered, like several others, that it had a serious design fault. The new version, which incorporated a reduced lower wing similar to that found on Nieuport fighters, suffered from random cases of wing failure. A few days after Richthofen's incident, all D.III fighters were grounded pending reinforcement of their lower wings with braces.[42] Richthofen switched over to one of *Jasta* 11's Halberstadt fighters before traveling to Berlin in early February to discuss the wing failure problem with authorities there. Before returning to *Jasta* 11, however, he had a quick visit with his mother:

"It's still early, the house sleeps, the bitter cold makes it good to be in bed. I believe I hear knocking. I turn on the light, the clock shows 7:00 in the morning. Suddenly, the door opens and Manfred is standing in front of my bed, fresh and happy, with no sign of fatigue following the long ride at night. The blue star glistens on his neck – the *Pour le Mérite*. I take his hand and speak as if praising a boy: 'Bravo, you've done well, Manfred.' I ask: 'How did you get in? Was the garden gate open?' No, it wasn't, but that didn't matter. The knight of the *Orden Pour le Mérite* had climbed over the fence."[43]

It was during this visit that Richthofen disclosed to his mother that he had painted his plane *"leuchtend rot"* ("bright red"). His autobiography made it sound as if the decision had been fanciful:

"For some reason, the thought occurred to me one day to paint my crate bright red. The result was that everyone absolutely couldn't help but notice my red bird. In fact, even my opponents weren't completely unaware of it."[44] But from what we know of Richthofen elsewhere, he did not appear to be a man prone to whimsy. His mother said he gave this reason: "'You can't really make yourself invisible in the air, so at least our people can recognize me.'" Brother Lothar gave what is probably a more realistic explanation, however:

"How did *Rittmeister* Richthofen come to paint his crate red? The French reported it as childish in an article. The reason can be sought elsewhere. When Manfred started to achieve his first victories with *Jasta* Boelcke, he was annoyed that the enemy spotted him far too early in air combat. He tried to make himself as undetectable as possible by using a variety of colors. He painted himself with different earth colors. One can't detect such a color from

Right: *Generaloberst* Ludwig von Falkenhausen, commander of the German 6th Army to which *Jasta* 11 was attached at the time, visits Richthofen at La Brayelle. Other photos tell us that the site was a small building at the edge of the airfield that Richthofen used as his command post. The same image was published in a c.8 April 1917 newspaper (*Illustrierte Kriegs-Zeitung* 140, p.8) that identified Richthofen as an *Oberleutnant* (promoted 23 March) who had recently gained his 30th success (24 March), so it is believed the photo was taken in late March 1917.

above as long as the thing [it was painted on] wasn't moving. To his sorrow, Manfred learned that no one color was useful. There's just no camouflage that can make an aviator invisible. Then, in order to at least always be recognizable by his comrades in the air as the lead plane, he chose the color bright red."[45] So the popular conception that he painted his plane red to flaunt himself before his enemies is incorrect. In fact, he had initially tried to accomplish the opposite. But when he understood that there was no way to conceal himself, he decided he might as well make it easier for his men to know where their leader was.

Evidently, it helped because Richthofen's leadership and instructions soon began to have a positive effect. *Vzfw.* Sebastian Festner was the first of his men to register a victory on 5 February. Festner scored again, along with *Lt.* Carl Allmenröder, on the 16th. They were joined by *Lt.* Karl-Emil Schaefer on 4 March and *Lt.* Kurt Wolff on 6 March. By the end of that month, *Jasta* 11 had amassed 36 confirmed kills, 15 by Richthofen himself and the remaining 21 spread among six other pilots.[46] Their closest competitor during the same timeframe was Richthofen's old unit, *Jasta* Boelcke, with 30 total victories (19 by *Lt.* Werner Voss). But the best was yet to come.

Bloody April

March 1917 had been a good month for Richthofen for two additional reasons. First, his younger brother, Lothar, had joined *Jasta* 11 on the 6th. Second, he

Above: *GenLt.* Ernst von Hoeppner, Commanding General of the Army Air Force, visited *Jasta* 11 on 23 April 1917 at Roucourt airfield to congratulate its members on having achieved their 100th victory the day before. Left to right: *Hptm.* Maximilian Sorg (Aviation Officer, 6th Army), Richthofen, Hoeppner, *Lt.* von Hartmann, *Lt.* Constantin Krefft, *Lt.* Karl-Emil Schaefer, *Lt.* Otto Brauneck, *Lt.* Lothar von Richthofen, *Lt.* Karl Esser.

had been promoted to *Oberleutnant* on the 23rd. This was superceded just two weeks later on 7 April when he was raised to *Rittmeister*. This incredibly rapid set of promotions was not only a reflection of the esteem in which he was held by his superiors but also a sure sign of their faith in his leadership abilities. They would not be disappointed.

The Germans, who were now fielding new Albatros D.III fighters against Great Britain's older stable of planes, took full advantage of their technological edge in April 1917. *Jasta* 11 was at the forefront of this effort and produced results like no other fighter squadron before or after them in the war. They were credited with no less than 89 victories that month with Manfred von Richthofen

contributing 21, Kurt Wolff surpassing his CO's count with 22, Lothar von Richthofen and Karl-Emil Schaefer with 15 each, Sebastian Festner 10, and Constantin Krefft and Georg Simon with 1 each. This unparalleled achievement resulted in a visit by their boss, *GenLt.* Ernst von Hoeppner, on 23 April to personally congratulate them on their 100th overall victory. There was also widespread newspaper coverage of them, complete with multiple photographs taken at their airfield. They quickly became national heroes. Postcards featuring their images were sold across Germany and newspapers began to follow their exploits on an almost daily basis. National accolades followed with *Lt.* Karl-Emil Schaefer becoming the first of Richthofen's

Above: Richthofen uses another mode of conveyance in front of one of *Jasta* 11's Albatros D.IIIs during a visit by his father on 29 April 1917. Left to right: *Oblt.* Wolfgang Plüschow, Richthofen, *Lt.* Lothar von Richthofen, *Lt.* von Hartmann, unknown, *Lt.* Karl Esser, *Lt.* Otto Brauneck, *Maj.* Albrecht von Richthofen, unknown. Note the airplane on its nose in the background between Brauneck and father Richthofen.

protégés to earn the *Pour le Mérite* on 26 April.

As their leader, Manfred von Richthofen was the most famous of them all. His mother noted in her diary:

"He's in all the newspapers, everyone is talking about him; a banner waves above his name. Cities honor him, royalty send telegraphs. No sooner have the congratulations arrived when a new victory chases the flag up the flagpole. It is unbelievable. The enemy is completely flustered."[47]

Some believed "the enemy" were more than flustered. A story began circulating that the British had formed a special "Anti-Richthofen Squadron" to dispense with him. Either in response to this or just due to growing concern, his men decided to adopt a predominantly red color scheme on their aircraft as well so that their leader would not be so conspicuous.[48] Schaefer added black markings to distinguish his plane, Allmenröder white, Wolff green and Lothar von Richthofen yellow. Manfred's

remained the only all-red plane, however.

Awards poured in for Richthofen from Germany's kingdoms: the Military Merit Order from Württemberg on 13 April, the Military St. Henry Order from Saxony on 16 April, and the Military Merit Order from Bavaria on 29 April. Nothing showed his elevated status more, however, than when he was summoned to the Kaiser's war court at Bad Kreuznach at the beginning of his May leave. On the 2nd, he was introduced to *Generalfeldmarschall* Paul von Hindenburg and his chief of staff, *General der Infanterie* Erich Ludendorff, then sent to the Kaiser's residence to have lunch with him. There, in honor of his 25th birthday, he received a bust of the Kaiser and sat on his right – the place of honor – during the meal. Then it was Hindenburg's turn to host Richthofen at a dinner that evening:

"No less than eight knights of the *Pour le Mérite* sat there together at table. I'll probably never see so many together in one bunch again, unless the war

Above: Manfred (left), Albrecht (center), and Lothar von Richthofen pose for the camera in front of the back entrance to Chateau Roucourt on 29 April 1917.

Above: One of several pictures taken during Richthofen's 1 May 1917 stopover in Cologne on his way to see his emperor in Bad Kreuznach. *Lt.* Constantin Krefft (left) flew him there in Rumpler C.I 1859/15.

lasts so long that the *Pour le Mérite* is diminished to the level of the Iron Cross 2nd Class."[49]

The next day, Richthofen was shuttled to Bad Homburg vor der Höhe where he was personally greeted by, and dined with, *Kaiserin* Auguste Victoria, who presented him with a gold and white cigarette case inscribed with her name. Having now been feted by his country's highest leaders, Richthofen was allowed some personal time and went on a brief hunting trip outside of Freiburg im Breisgau. While there, he learned that another of his *Jasta* 11 pupils, *Lt.* Kurt Wolff, had been given the *Pour le Mérite* on 4 May as well as a command of his own, *Jasta* 29. Berlin was Richthofen's next stop where he had official business with the *Inspektion der Fliegertruppe (Idflieg)* that included a test flight of a proposed new fighter, the LFG Roland D.III. Leery of the Albatros D.III's history of lower wing

Facing Page, Bottom: Kaiser Wilhelm II (spiked helmet) leaves his headquarters building at Bad Kreuznach as Richthofen (second from right) bows in deference to him.

Above: *Generalfeldmarschall* Paul von Hindenburg (center) is saluted as *GenLt*. Ernst von Hoeppner (to the right of Hindenburg) and *Oberstlt*. Hermann Thomsen (further right with scabbard) accompany him away from one of their 2 May 1917 meetings. Richthofen is in the background, fourth from right.

Above: While in Berlin, Richthofen enjoyed some time off at the Mehl-Mühlens Races at nearby Grunewald on 16 May 1917. Here he stands at the racetrack next to someone identified as "Prinz Friedrich von Preussen," who may have been Friedrich Leopold, younger brother of princes Friedrich Sigismund and Friedrich Karl of Prussia.

failure, he was only too glad to oblige. Before the test flight, however, Richthofen received both bad and good news about his brother. The bad news was that Lothar had been seriously wounded in the hip by ground fire on 13 May. The good news was that he was in stable condition in a Douai hospital and was expected to recover fully. Moreover, he had been decorated with the *Pour le Mérite* on 14 May. Relieved of his duties and reassured by Lothar's prognosis, Richthofen was finally able to head home on an 18 May overnight train that reached Schweidnitz the next morning.

Home Leave

"Ilse picked Manfred up from the station on Saturday at seven in the morning. They got here on foot. The news of his arrival had scarcely spread when a flood of flower bouquets and small gifts rained down on us. The entire city seemed mobilized. I knew how strongly opposed Manfred was to being feted. But nothing could be done about it now, and he reluctantly reconciled himself to his role. Nothing was missing from these ovations,

neither the *Wandervogel* [back to nature youth movement] with their buzzing lute chants nor the preschool children with little paper helmets and tassels. The beautiful weather on Sunday encouraged a mass migration to our home. At times, the street was black with people. Everyone wanted to see him. We remained in the garden all day. Deputations came and went. The *Jung-Deutschland* [literary and political movement] – the *Jugendwehr* [premilitary training group] – the *Volksschule* [public elementary school] – speeches – serenades – speeches – the municipal authorities sent a young oak tree garnished with Marshall Neil roses; military bands blared... In the evening, we could no longer stand due to fatigue."[50]

As Richthofen himself wryly put it: "On the whole, it became clear to me that the homeland still has a lively interest in its soldiers in the field."[51]

Richthofen was visited in Schweidnitz by a stenographer from Berlin's Verlag Ullstein & Co. who spent several days recording the stories that served as the basis for his autobiography, *Der rote Kampfflieger*. When two local women encountered

Above: Richthofen flew to Breslau on his way to Militsch on 31 May 1917, where this photograph was probably taken of him meeting up with his former CO at *Kasta* 8, *Hptm*. Viktor Carganico (left). See pages 76–77 below for additional photos taken then.

them both entering his home and appeared to be overly inquisitive, he introduced the stenographer with utmost seriousness as "my fiancée." His mother recalled:

"I stood in the garden and watched as the attractive Berliner bit her lips, and I too started to laugh. The ladies, on the other hand – with the guarded mistrust that usually accompanies nosiness – turned around quite cooly and rushed off."[52]

After finishing his dictations, he went to Pless (now Pszczyna, Poland) for another hunting excursion – courtesy of Hans Heinrich XI, Prince of Pless – arriving there on 26 May. A few days later, he returned to Schweidnitz and was collected there on the last day of the month to begin a tour of Austro-Hungarian and Ottoman aviation facilities. Richthofen abruptly ended the tour and returned

from Vienna after he learned that *Lt.* Karl-Emil Schaefer had been killed in combat on 5 June. Schaefer had been given command of *Jasta* 28 on 27 April and, like Richthofen and Boelcke before him, had led his unit by example, adding another 7 victories to bring his total to 30 before his death. Richthofen arranged to fly to his comrade's funeral service that was held in Krefeld on 11 June, and then stayed on two days to visit former *Jasta* 2/Boelcke comrade *Lt.* Werner Voss and his family.[53] Richthofen returned to Bad Kreuznach to attend more functions with the Kaiser, Hindenburg, Ludendorff, and Czar Ferdinand of Bulgaria, who took the opportunity to personally award Richthofen with his Bravery Order, 4th Class. Afterwards, he visited brother Lothar in Seclin where he was being treated for his hip wound by Professor Dr. Burkhard.[54]

Above: Richthofen (third from right) holds a conversation at an airfield, date and place unknown. *Lt.* Constantin Krefft is at far left, mostly obscured by *Lt.* Kurt Wolff (hands behind back). Other photos taken at the same time show Wolff wearing his *Pour le Mérite* (awarded 4 May 1917) and Richthofen does not show any signs of the head wound he suffered on 6 July, so this image probably occurred in May or June 1917.

Then it was back to the front on 17 June; but not before the news reached him that yet a fourth of his protégés, *Lt.* Carl Allmenröder, had joined the ranks of the knights of the *Orden Pour le Mérite* on 14 June.

Jagdgeschwader Commander

While in Berlin, Richthofen had learned that he was to be placed in charge of Germany's first fighter wing, *Jagdgeschwader Nr.1* (*JG* 1). It was initially scheduled to consist of *Jastas* 6, 7, 11, and 26, but 7 and 26 were replaced by *Jastas* 4 and 10 when it was officially formed on 24 June. The next day, when Richthofen downed his 56th victim, his formal appointment as *Geschwaderführer* came through. Preparations were then made to assemble the new fighter wing at Markebeke (near Kortrijk), Belgium.

While this was taking place, Richthofen took time off to visit his brother who was now recuperating in Hamburg. There he learned that another of his star pupils, *Lt.* Carl Allmenröder, had died on 27

June having nosedived, apparently unconscious, into no-man's-land.[55] Richthofen returned to Kortrijk for Allmenröder's 1 July memorial service, where he was joined by *Lt.* Kurt Wolff, who had been recalled to *Jasta* 11. Richthofen put on a brave front in his letter to Allmenröder's father, closing with: "I myself could not wish for a more beautiful death than falling in air combat; it is a comfort to know that Carl felt nothing at the end."[56] He was more candid, however, with Allmenröder's brother Wilhelm, who had briefly served in *Jasta* 11 before being wounded: "Tears still spring to my eyes whenever I remember that this fine example of a man is no longer among the living."[57]

There was little time for mourning, however, and Richthofen returned his attention to *JG* 1, which officially began its operations as a unit on 6 July. That morning, as Richthofen's flight engaged a group of FE.2d's from RFC No.20 Squadron, A6512's observer, 2Lt. Albert E. Woodbridge, opened fire at Richthofen's Albatros from a distance of 300 meters.

Right: Richthofen began a tour of Austro-Hungarian aviation facilities in early June 1917 that he ended upon hearing the news of *Lt*. Karl-Emil Schaefer's death on 5 June. This rare photo shows him during that tour in company with several unknown Austro-Hungarian officers. Note that Richthofen is displaying two decorations from their kingdom: the Army Field Pilot's Badge (on right breast) and the Military Merit Cross, 3rd Class with War Decoration (just below his *Pour le Mérite*).

Above: Richthofen, accompanied by war correspondent *Hptm*. Erich von Saltzmann, flew from Berlin to Krefeld and arrived just in time for the funeral held there on 11 June 1917 for his comrade, *Lt*. Karl-Emil Schaefer. After the ceremony, Richthofen stayed on for a brief visit with *Lt*. Werner Voss and his family. Here he is saying goodbye to Max Voss Sr., Werner's father, before returning to Cologne in his borrowed Albatros C.III 2309/16.

Above: On his way back to the front in mid-June 1917, Richthofen visited his brother Lothar (left) at a Seclin hospital. Father Albrecht, who had an administrative post near Lille, dropped by as well.

Richthofen watched as his intended prey's pilot, Capt. Douglas C. Cunnell, turned and headed toward him, adding the fire of his side-mounted machine gun to that of his observer's nose-mounted one:

"Then, all of a sudden, a blow to my head! I was hit! For a moment, my entire body was completely paralyzed. My hands hung down, my legs dangled in the cockpit. The worst thing was that my optic nerve had been affected by the blow to my head and I was completely blind. The machine dove down. For a moment, it went through my head: so this is what it's like when one is going down and is about to die. I expected that the wings wouldn't be able

to withstand the dive and would break off at any moment."[58]

Gradually, however, Richthofen regained the use of his hands and feet, and then black and white specks started to appear before his eyes. His sight was returning. By the time that he could see his altimeter and its 800 meter reading, he was able to reduce power, pull out of his dive, and flatten out. He couldn't land immediately because he was still above a landscape filled with shell holes. Then he noticed two of his comrades, *Lt.* Otto Brauneck and *Lt.* Alfred Niederhoff, who had kept watch over him as he fell and were now accompanying him.

Above: On 17 June 1917, Richthofen was transported from Cologne to Courtrai (Kortrijk) by *Lt.* Guido Scheffer in Albatros C.III 4057/16. This is one of several photos taken on that occasion. Scheffer is at far left, next to Richthofen. Scheffer was subsequently asked to join *Jasta* 11, which he did on 12 July 1917.

"So I gave it gas again and flew towards the east at low altitude, while I still maintained consciousness. Initially, all went quite well. But after a few seconds I noticed that my strength was waning and that it was gradually growing black before my eyes again. Now it was high time. I landed and was even able to set down smoothly, taking some posts and telephone lines with me, which really didn't matter to me at the time. I still had the strength to stand up in my machine and wanted to climb out; but I fell out, and no longer having the strength to stand, laid myself right down."[59]

Richthofen had set down in a field near Wervicq, Belgium. He was taken to Field Hospital 76 in Kortrijk, where Prof.Dr. Kraske discovered that a glancing blow had removed a patch of skin on his head about 10 centimeters in diameter.[60] The bullet had not penetrated his skull, but had left him with a serious concussion – an affliction from which many believe he never fully recovered. Nonetheless, he fought through the pain and discomfort and resumed command of *JG* 1 on 25 July, less than three weeks after he had narrowly escaped death.

Richthofen was not allowed to fly, but could at least try to improve the lot of those that could. He

had grown to despise the Albatros D.V type that he had only begun to fly in late June and was actively seeking its replacement. He believed a new Fokker design was the answer and promised his men: "You will receive the new Fokker triplane, which climbs like a monkey and is as agile as the Devil."[61]

He also brought in star fighter pilot *Lt.* Werner Voss, with 34 victories and the *Pour le Mérite*, to supplement *JG* 1's roster as *Jasta* 10's new CO. When Richthofen was finally able to climb into an airplane again on 16 August, he must have been proud of the fact that during his absence, *JG* 1 had managed to amass a total of 83 victories. He also demonstrated that he had not lost his touch by shooting down a Nieuport fighter that day for his 58th official kill. After word of this reached his superiors, he received a telegram from *GenLt.* Ernst von Hoeppner that both congratulated and admonished him: "With regard to *Rittmeister Freiherr* von Richthofen, who I cordially congratulate on his 58th air victory, I expect that he is aware of the responsibility of deploying his own person and that – until he has overcome the last vestiges of his wound – he will fly only when absolute necessity justifies it."[62] Richthofen's response was his 59th victory on 26

Above: *Maj.* Albrecht von Richthofen (left) visits with his wounded son.

August. He stubbornly persisted in taking to the air even though the effort cost him physically, if not mentally. He confided to his mother on 28 August:

"I'm very pleased about Lothar's health. But under no circumstances should he return to the front before he is completely physically fit. Otherwise, he'll become worn out and be shot down. I know best from my own experience. I've made only two flights against the enemy, and although both met with success, I was completely exhausted after each flight. I almost got sick after the first. My wound is healing terribly slowly; it's still as big as a five Mark piece. Yesterday, they removed a bone splinter; I think it will be the last."[63]

The Fokker Triplane
On the same day that he wrote the letter above to his mother, two pre-production Fokker triplanes,

Above: A recuperating Richthofen (with bandaged head) dines with his men at Chateau Béthune outside of Markebeke. Seated next to him, facing the camera, is *Oblt*. Wilhelm Reinhard, who would go on to command *JG* 1 following Richthofen's death. *Oblt*. Karl Bodenschatz (*JG* 1's adjutant) is directly opposite Richthofen next to *Lt*. Eberhardt Mohnicke. Note that the men are being serenaded by a band (at right).

Above: These two images display how the dressing covering Richthofen's head wound was kept in place. They were taken outside of Chateau Béthune sometime between 31 August and 3 September.

34

Above: Richthofen (center) shares a light moment with the dignitaries who visited Markebeke airfield on 31 August 1917. German Chancellor Georg Michaelis (light overcoat) is in the front row two men over to the right from Richthofen, followed by Gen. Sixt von Arnim.

F.I 102/17 and 103/17, were delivered to Markebeke airfield for assessment by Richthofen and *Lt.* Werner Voss, respectively. Richthofen had made this complaint after canceling an intercept mission on 10 August:

"Reason: the English bombing and reconnaissance squadrons now fly over our lines at very high altitude (4,500 to 5,000 meters). Our machines do not have sufficient climbing ability to reach the enemy in time."[64]

To stop the enemy, you had to get up to them first and Richthofen was counting on the triplane to help *JG* 1 do that. What it lacked in top speed, it more than made up for in climb rate and maneuverability – two essential qualities that Richthofen found lacking in the Albatros D.V. On 31 August, he showed his new mount off at Markebeke to a group of visiting dignitaries that included the recently appointed *Reichskanzler* (Chancellor of Germany) Georg Michaelis. Anthony Fokker was on hand to take photographs and movies of the event. Richthofen took the plane out for its first combat mission the next day, but he did not get much of a chance to put it to the test because as he approached his intended victim he was evidently mistaken for a Sopwith triplane. Richthofen came right up to his prey and shot him down while the observer never

made a move to man his gun.

Richthofen's 61st, two days later, was a much different story:

"Involved along with five *Jasta* 11 aircraft in a squadron fight against English single-seaters, I took on one of the opponents at 3,500 meters altitude and forced him to land near Bousbecque after a rather long dogfight. I was absolutely convinced that I was facing a very skillful airman, who didn't give up even at 50 meters altitude, but continued to shoot, and even while flattening out to land fired at an infantry column and then intentionally rolled his machine up against a tree. The Fokker triplane F.I 102/17 was absolutely superior to the English Sopwith."[65]

Richthofen's opponent had been RFC No.46 Squadron's Lt. Algernon Bird in Sopwith Pup B1795.Z. Bird was not only skilled but plucky as well, evidently not caring to ingratiate himself to the people who were about to take him prisoner. Anthony Fokker, still at Markebeke, filmed Richthofen inspecting the downed plane and standing with an understandably uncomfortable Bird before he was taken off to prison. The film of the event that also includes other shots of Richthofen and F.I 102/17 can still be viewed today.[66]

Obviously, the new triplane had lived up to Richthofen's expectations and was more than

Above: The group enjoys a flying display overhead. *Oblt.* Karl Bodenschatz (facing camera) is in the left foreground. Richthofen (with dressing strap on head) is over to the right, followed by Michaelis and Arnim at far right.

battle worthy. Demonstrating that fact, however, cost Richthofen. As *JG* 1's adjutant, *Oblt.* Karl Bodenschatz, reported, his commander's recent victories made it clear that he was not complying with *GenLt.* Ernst von Hoeppner's wishes. On 6 September, this "had serious repercussions: the *Rittmeister* begins a 'voluntary' four-week leave – compulsory and vigorously pushed by everyone in high places."[67]

Once again, Anthony Fokker's camera was on hand to witness the transfer of command of *JG* 1 from Richthofen to *Oblt.* Kurt von Döring. It also captured Richthofen upon his departure in an all-red Albatros C.IX that appears to have served as the fighter wing's transport plane.[68] Richthofen had been grounded, so *Jasta* 11's *Lt.* Eberhardt Mohnicke sat up front as his pilot.

Before going home, Richthofen traveled to Friedrichroda as the guest of Carl Eduard, Duke of Saxe-Coburg-Gotha, where he hunted and roamed the grounds of the duke's Reinhardsbrunn Castle for several weeks. The idyllic surroundings were invaded by the war's harsh reality when word reached Richthofen that *Lt.* Kurt Wolff – the man they kiddingly nicknamed the *"zarte Blümlein"*

("gentle little flower") in direct contrast to his "Berserker" ("warrior seized by battle frenzy") nature in combat – had been killed in combat on 15 September.[69] Moreover, he had been shot down while flying Richthofen's F.I 102/17. Richthofen issued a heartfelt obituary for his comrade and tried to return to his rest and relaxation.[70] But more bad news followed. *Lt.* Werner Voss – the comrade who had come closest to Richthofen's tally of 61 with 48 of his own – was brought down on 23 September in what many consider to have been the epic dogfight of the war.

Richthofen took a train to Berlin and then flew to Schweidnitz, where he arrived on 9 October.[71] There the family enjoyed what turned out to be their final joint reunion, with Albrecht, Lothar, and younger brother Bolko (a cadet) also returning home. Richthofen's mother wrote that she was horrified to discover that his head wound had still not healed and that a small amount of bone remained exposed. She also noted that he sometimes suffered severe headaches and was uncharacteristically irritable for much of the time. His superiors had been right: he had gone back into the fight prematurely and still required further rest and recuperation.

Above: A picture of Richthofen during one of his hunting jaunts, date and place unknown.

But Richthofen had also learned that bad things happened to his comrades when he was away from the front. Lothar had been wounded and Schaefer and Allmenröder both killed during his absence in May and June; more recently, it had been Wolff and Voss who had died. Richthofen was awarded five decorations during his enforced leave, something he might have reacted to as 'twisting the knife' during a time when his comrades were fighting and dying without him.[72] A certain amount of 'survivor's guilt' can be perceived behind the response he gave to his mother's request that he quit flying: "Would you be pleased if I brought myself to safety now and rested on my laurels?"[73] His sense of duty and loyalty to his comrades prevented him from understanding that that is precisely what she would have liked.

Restless, but still in need of rest, Richthofen went on another hunting sojourn to Ottau (now in the Czech Republic). Then either he or his superiors finally had enough. He returned to *JG* 1 on 23 October and soon climbed back up into the air. He had a new triplane, Dr.I 114/17, and was flying it a week later on 30 October when the engine on his brother Lothar's triplane suddenly quit. Lothar was left with no choice but to descend immediately for

an emergency landing. Richthofen followed him down and watched as he made a smooth touchdown near Zilverberg. He then tried to land alongside his brother but ran into some difficulty and crashed. Though uninjured, Richthofen was shocked by the damage to his plane that was much more extensive than it should have been and had rendered 114/17 as a total write-off. That same day, veteran ace *Lt.* Heinrich Gontermann was killed when the top wing of his 115/17 triplane collapsed in midair. Then *Jasta* 11's *Lt.* Günther Pastor met with the same fate a day later. Obviously, something was wrong with the new design and *Idflieg's Zentral-Abnahme-Kommission* (Central Acceptance Commission) was called in to investigate. Their findings – structural deficiencies coupled with poor workmanship – grounded the triplanes until replacement wings that corrected those problems could be fitted to them. So it was back to the inferior Albatros D.V and Pfalz D.III fighters.

Facing Page: A portrait of Manfred von Richthofen in flight gear.

Above: The brothers Richthofen (Manfred at far left, Lothar two men over from him) take a stroll with two other officers.

Transfer and Fighting Hiatus

JG 1 was transferred to the Cambrai region (*JG* 1 and *Jasta* 11 were based at Avesnes-le-Sec, *Jastas* 4 and 6 at Lieu-Saint-Amand, and *Jasta* 10 at Iwuy) immediately after the major offensive was opened by the British there on 20 November. Richthofen led his fighter wing on its first sortie in the new sector on 23 November and achieved his 62nd victory. Then came the depressing news of *Lt.* Erwin Böhme's death in combat on 29 November. On 1 December, the day Richthofen's 63rd victim fell, he set about the mournful task of writing a letter of condolence to Böhme's brother Gerhard:

"I just received the painful news of your brother's death. One becomes firm and hard in war, but I nevertheless took this case close to heart – You yourself know how close your brother stood in friendship to me. On the last afternoon before his death, he was here with me at Avesnes le Sec – my new airdrome – full of joy over the development of our dear old *Jagdstaffel* Boelcke, which has been led back to its former heights solely and entirely due to him. Now they are both united in Valhalla: your splendid brother and his great master to whom, of us all, he was closest."[74]

When the Battle of Cambrai ended on 7 December, so did Richthofen's combat activities until the following spring. First he traveled to the Pfalz factory works at Speyer on 12 December to inspect and test their triplane design. It appears that he was not overly impressed with the type and a disappointed Richthofen returned to *JG* 1's command on 20 December. Right after a Christmas spent with Lothar and father Albrecht, the Richthofen brothers departed on a trip to Brest

Litovsk (now Brest, Belarus) where they had been invited by Prince Leopold of Bavaria to take part in the peace negotiations being held there following Russia's ceasefire declaration of 15 December. Both men soon learned that they were little more than window dressing, however, so they took a break to hunt together during their stay. After their return, Richthofen was almost placed at the same dining table as the Russian delegation's Anastasia Bitsenko, who had just been released from prison for the murder of a Russian general in 1905. Richthofen mused:

"It would have been a grand, amusing conversation. I was very much looking forward to it because she too had hunted down some of her enemies. Even though they were ministers and grand dukes and the like, for which she had been banished to a prison in Siberia, it at least would have been the starting point for a conversation."[75]

Richthofen next traveled to Berlin where he attended the fighter trial competition that began on 21 January at Adlershof field. It was the first time that the military had hosted such an event where all the major aircraft manufacturers (e.g., AEG, Albatros, Aviatik, DFW, Fokker, Junkers, Kondor, LVG, Pfalz, Roland, Rumpler, Schütte-Lanz, Siemens-Schukert) gathered at one venue to offer up their fighter plane prototypes for evaluation. Richthofen had successfully promoted the concept that front line pilots needed to be included in order to give their own assessments of how the different types might perform in the field, so he was there along with other accomplished airmen such as *Lt.* Hans Klein (recent *Pour le Mérite* recipient and CO of *Jasta* 10 with 22 victories), *Hptm.* Adolf *Ritter* von Tutschek (former CO of *Jasta* 12 who would be named *Geschwaderführer* of *JG* 2 on 1 February, 23 victories), *Oblt.* Bruno Loerzer (CO of *Jasta* 26 who would lead *JG* 3 on 21 February, 22 victories), *Lt.* Josef Jacobs (CO of *Jasta* 7, 12 victories) and *Lt.* Erich Loewenhardt (*Jasta* 10, 10 victories). Fokker and his movie camera captured several scenes of the airmen playfully joking with each other as well as another featuring Tutschek in Fokker's V.11 prototype that Richthofen test flew as well. The V.11, the predecessor of what would become the highly successful D.VII, was eventually selected for mass production.

Richthofen had other duties in Berlin, such as visiting and talking with striking munitions workers. A lighter moment came when he went to Schulte's Art Gallery to view a painting done of him by acclaimed artist Fritz Reusing in 1917:

"An elderly gentleman came up and stood beside him. Richthofen said to him, 'I beg your pardon

Above: A *JG* 1 lineup for the camera. Left to right: *Lt.* Hans-Georg von der Osten, *Lt.* Werner Steinhäuser, *Lt.* Siegfried Gussmann, *Lt.* Karl-August von Schoenebeck, unknown, *Lt.* Lothar von Richthofen, *Rittm.* Manfred von Richthofen, *Lt.* Guido Scheffer, *Lt.* Constantin Krefft, *Oblt.* Karl Bodenschatz, *Lt.* Hans-Karl von Linsingen, *Lt.* Hans-Joachim Wolff, *Oblt.* Hans-Helmuth von Boddien, *Lt.* Johann Janzen, *Lt.* Erich Just. We can be fairly certain that the photo was taken in the first half of December 1917 because Werner Steinhäuser arrived that month and Guido Scheffer left for *FEA* 6 on the 18th.

but I am told that I have some likeness to this painting!' The gentleman put on his spectacles, took a look at the picture, took a look at Richthofen, and finally said, 'I think you can forget that notion.' Ten minutes later Richthofen joined us at the hotel, beaming with joy, and related the incident."[76]

Privately, however, such humorous moments could do little to dispel the gloom brought on by years of war, the loss of so many friends, and the sense of mortality engendered by his wound. Richthofen wrote:

"I write this down without knowing if anyone other than my next of kin will ever get to see this transcript. I am thinking about writing a continuation of the *Red Combat Pilot,* and indeed, for a very particular reason. The struggle that is now taking place on all fronts has become damnably serious; there is nothing left of the 'bright, merry war' as our deeds were called at first. Now we have to defend ourselves everywhere with the greatest desperation so that the enemy doesn't violate our country. I now have the dismal impression that the *Red Combat Pilot* projected a much different Richthofen to people than how I really am and feel. When I read the book, I smile at how flippant I was. Now I no longer feel so flippant. Not because

Above: Richthofen in deep conversation with *Oblt.* Hans Bethge, CO of *Jasta* 30.

I can imagine how it will be one day when death is breathing down my neck – surely not that, even though I've been reminded often enough that one

Left: On 10 March 1918, Richthofen attended the funeral services that were held for *Jasta* 11's *Lt.* Erich Bahr, killed in action on 6 March. In this graveside image, Richthofen can be seen in the background just in front of the pastor with *Oblt.* Karl Bodenschatz to the right.

day that could happen. People in high places have told me that I should give up flying because it'll catch up with me some day. I would be miserable with myself, however, if now, full of glory and decorations, I were to exist as a pensioner of my own dignity in order to preserve my precious life for the nation, while every poor fellow in the trenches, doing his duty just as I am, perseveres. I feel wretched after each air combat; however, that's probably the result of my head wound. When I step back onto the ground at my airfield, I go straight for the four walls [of my room], don't want to see anyone or hear anything. I think it's really not like the people at home imagine, with cheers and shouting; it's all much more serious, grim…"[77]

When Richthofen finally went home again for a brief visit at the end of the January, his mother also noticed that he was no longer the same man:

"He was serious – very serious – and quiet. I found that Manfred had changed quite a bit overall. Though he looked better and more rested than he did during his fall leave, his soul lacked merriment, lightheartedness, high-spiritedness. He was taciturn and turned away, almost unapproachable; each word seemed to come from some far off place… I thought: he has seen death too often… Manfred had to go for

dental treatment to undergo some minor, everyday treatment. Then he said half aloud to himself – but I heard it nevertheless: 'Actually, there's really no point in it anymore…'"[78]

Deeply concerned, his mother concluded: "I had never seen him like this before and didn't recognize him."[79] When Richthofen departed for Berlin a few days later, she called after him with the words: "Goodbye – until we meet again, my boy."[80] She had no way of knowing that that would never – at least on this earth – happen again.

The Final Months and Day

German High Command had been discussing a spring 1918 offensive since November 1917. In early 1918, Russia's withdrawal from the war afforded them the opportunity to move numerous divisions from the Eastern Front to the Western Front, which they began to do in February. Richthofen, who had returned to the front around the same time, grew frustrated with the lack of air fighting and complained that he was leading four ground support units rather than a fighter wing. This all changed in March, however, when the British stepped up their efforts to obtain more information on the German buildup. Back to flying the Fokker Dr.I, Richthofen

Above: A few days later, on 13 March 1918, Richthofen flew over to *Jasta* 5 and went to the memorial service for that unit's *Lt.* Wilhelm Gürke, killed in action on 10 March. Here Richthofen is at far left followed by *Jasta* 5 CO *Oblt.* Richard Flashar, the presiding pastor, unknown, *Lt.* Hans-Joachim von Hippel, *Oblt.* Zettemeyer, unknown, *Hptm.* Wilhelm Haehnelt (Aviation Officer, 2nd Army).

brought down his 64th opponent on 12 March and his 65th the next day. He could have been knocked off his stride when Lothar was wounded and crashed yet again during the latter engagement; but instead, once he was satisfied that his brother was going to recover, he appeared to take to the skies with renewed vigor. He brought down another plane on 18 March. Then on 20 March, the day before Operation Michael commenced, *JG* 1 was positioned further west near Awoingt to bring it closer to the front lines. From there, Richthofen added another two to his tally. As the offensive progressed and gained ground, *JG* 1 was moved forward to an airfield near Léchelle on 26 March, where he achieved another 10 victories, including two on the 26th and three on the 27th, to bring his total to 78. In recognition of his unparalleled 70th success, he was accorded a singular honor on 6 April when the Kaiser bestowed him with the Red Eagle Order, 3rd Class with Crown and Swords, normally reserved for officers of lieutenant colonel or higher rank. It was one of only two such wartime awards and was the only instance where it was granted to an airman. After the fighter

wing was advanced again to Cappy on 12 April, Richthofen scored a double on 20 April to bring his total to an even 80 – exactly twice what his mentor, Oswald Boelcke, had accomplished. Upon landing, he reportedly smacked his hands together and said: "Well well, 80 is quite a respectable number!"[81] Richthofen was back in form and beginning to look like he might approach the same stellar success he had enjoyed a year earlier.

Lt. Richard Wenzl, who had just joined *JG* 1's *Jasta* 11 on 27 March, recalled the events of 21 April in his book, *Richthofen-Flieger*:

"The morning of 21 April was somewhat foggy and very misty, resulting in almost no enemy air activity. After a short time, the east wind increased and it cleared up. We went to the field. Richthofen still wanted to wait for awhile, so that 'the English would get really cheeky.' He was in splendid humor. He had shot down his 79th and 80th the day before, and was openly happy about that. His leave had already been approved. He was going to fly together with Wölfchen [i.e., *Lt.* Hans-Joachim Wolff] to Freiburg im Breisgau on the 24th, and from there

Above: This and the next photograph are the "two photos" *Lt.* Richard Wenzl identified as the last taken of Richthofen alive. The first shows Richthofen consoling Moritz, who appears to have just been released from the rope tied to the wheel chock in the foreground. *Lt.* Erich Loewenhardt observes the scene at right. Some historians have pointed to the old style markings on the Dr.I behind them as an indication that the photo was taken earlier in March before the new *Balkenkreuz* insignia were put into effect. But we now know that virtually all Dr.Is were sent to the front with such markings well into May 1918 and had to be converted to the new *Balkenkreuz* insignia in the field. Moreover, *Jasta* 4 received its first triplanes on 20 April, so the Dr.I in the background may have been one of them, having just had its tail painted before moving on to converting its insignia.

go hunting in the Black Forest. All preparations had been made – a sleeper car ticket had even been acquired for him in case there was bad flying weather. Richthofen's mood rubbed off on the rest of us. Everyone was in good spirits. This gave rise to all sorts of mischief. Richthofen joined in. First he threw me down from a stretcher – I had only wanted to take a little snooze – and then others who tried to do the same thing. I decided to take some picures and got my apparatus [i.e., camera]. In the meantime, a joker had tied a wheel chock with a long rope to Moritz's (Richthofen's beloved dog!) tail. Richthofen called "Moritz" – who jumped up, and the poor creature dragged the chock around in circles, resigned to his fate. I used the moment to take two photos. They were the last of the old master."[82]

A few minutes later, around 11:00, two *Ketten* (flights) from *Jasta* 11 took to the air, one led by *Lt.* Hans Weiss, the other by Richthofen. When they returned to base about an hour later, Richthofen was not among them. Wenzl and Wolff both voiced their concern, having seen a red plane possibly in trouble below them far over the enemy lines. Wenzl, *Oblt.*

Walther Karjus, and *Lt.* Wolfram von Richthofen (a cousin) took off again to search for Richthofen but were driven away by ground fire and enemy aircraft. When they landed, they learned that reports had been made of a red triplane landing near the Bray-Corbie road in enemy territory; but Richthofen's fate was still unknown. After two days of anxious waiting, a Reuter newspaper report confirmed the worst. Richthofen had been shot down, killed by a single bullet that had traversed his lungs and punctured his heart.

During their final visit, Richthofen had shared this concern with his mother:

"I have nothing to fear in the air – not in the air. We can deal with them, even when there are so many of them... The worst that could happen to me is if I had to land on the other side."

He need not have worried, because in death at least, the British honored him, giving him a full military funeral at nearby Bertangles cemetery on 22 April.[83]

Life was over for Richthofen, but the controversy surrounding his death was just beginning. What we

Above: The metal huts, pointed Bell tents, power poles, and other paraphernalia in the background of this photo leave little doubt that this picture was taken at Cappy. Richthofen and Loewenhardt appear the same as they did in the prior photo. Nevertheless, some still question whether this picture was taken on 21 April 1918 as Wenzl stated. Left to right: *Lt.* Wolfram von Richthofen (Manfred's cousin), *Vzfw.* Edgar Scholtz, *Oblt.* Walther Karjus, *Lt.* Hans-Joachim Wolff, *Hptm.* Kurt Lischke, Richthofen, Loewenhardt, *Lt.* Werner Steinhäuser, *Lt.* Hans Weiss.

know for certain is that Richthofen and his men had run into a flight of red-nosed Sopwith Camels from RAF No.209 Squadron. He chased after D3326, piloted by 2Lt. Wilfred R. May, and both men came down low to the ground. At one point, Capt. A. Roy Brown dove on Richthofen's plane and fired. A short time after that, Richthofen's triplane was observed to turn back toward its own lines, stagger, and steeply glide to the earth near the Bray-Corbie Road. It ended up in a mangel (beet fertilizer) heap, and when Australian ground troops arrived at the scene, Richthofen was already dead. The English ruled that it had been Brown who had fired the fatal shot; and to this day, 209 Squadron's official crest includes a falling red eagle – a symbol of Richthofen's demise. But the ensuing years have rendered multiple, extensive studies of the evidence and most historians now believe that Richthofen was brought down by ground fire. Arguments have been presented for various machine gunners as having been the victor, but it is also possible that some anonymous soldier had delivered an either well-aimed or lucky blow.

A memorial service for Richthofen was held on what would have been his 26th birthday in Berlin's Garnisonkirche (now Kirche am Südstern).

Commanding General of the Air Force *GenLt.* Ernst von Hoeppner and a host of other dignitaries participated, and the Richthofen family was given the high honor of having Empress Auguste Victoria and her nephew, Prince Sigismund of Prussia, seated beside them. In 1921, Richthofen's remains were exhumed from Bertangles and reinterred at the German Military Cemetery outside of Fricourt.[84] They were subsequently returned to German soil and reburied at Berlin's Invalidenfriedhof cemetery on 20 November 1925. German President Paul von Hindenburg attended the elaborate state funeral in which no less than 17 *Pour le Mérite* recipients – Paul Bäumer, Oskar von Boenigk, Karl Bolle, Heinrich Bongartz, Julius Buckler, Carl Degelow, Alfred Keller, Hans Klein, Hermann Köhl, Otto Könnecke, Arthur Laumann, Leo Leonhardy, Bruno Loerzer, Josef Mai, Josef Veltjens, Franz Walz, Curt Wüsthoff – served as pallbearers and honor guards.[85] Years later, in 1975, the family quietly had Richthofen's remains transferred to a family plot at Südfriedhof cemetery in Wiesbaden, where Baroness Kunigunde's grave (died 24 April 1962) is surrounded by those of her children – Manfred, Ilse (†2 July 1963), Bolko (†3 December 1971) and a memorial plaque to Lothar (†4 July 1922).[86]

Above: An Australian honor guard fires a salute volley during Richthofen's funeral ceremony in Bertangles cemetery on 22 April. Richthofen was buried just inside the cemetery gates and the site is marked today for tourists.

Endnotes

[1] Richthofen referred to himself as *"Der rote Kampfflieger"* ("The Red Combat Pilot") in the title of his autobiography and also stated that the English called him *"Le petit rouge"* ("Little Red") early in his career. His mother said he was known as *"diable rouge"* ("red devil") among the French. An RAF No.209 Squadron 1918 Christmas card (see p.51) indicates that it was the British who later coined the term "The Red Baron" for Richthofen. Charles M. Schulz introduced "The Red Baron" as Snoopy's foe in October 1965 and Stanley Ulanoff adopted that as the title of his translation of *"Der rote Kampfflieger"* in 1969.

[2] *The Red Knight of Germany* (New York: Bantam Books, 1964), p.7.

[3] *Der rote Kampfflieger* (1917), p.12; for another translation, see *The Red Baron*, p.1.

[4] Ibid.

[5] *Der rote Kampfflieger* (1917), p.13; *The Red Baron*, p.2.

[6] *Der rote Kampfflieger* (1917), p.38; *The Red Baron*, pp.17–18 (but see next endnote).

[7] The original German text read: *"Die Mönche waren überaus liebenswürdig. Sie gaben uns zu essen und zu trinken, so viel wir haben wollten, und wir liessen es uns gut schmecken...Mit anderen Worten, wir richteten uns so ein, als ob wir im Manöver bei einem lieben Gastfreund zu Abend wären. Nebenbei bemerkt, hingen drei Tage darauf mehrere von den Gastgebern an dem Laternenpfahl, da sie es sich nicht hatten verkneifen können, sich an dem Krieg zu beteiligen. Aber an dem Abend waren sie wirklich überaus liebenswürdig."* Though *hingen* could technically be interpreted as "we hanged" instead of "were hanged," it should be noted that *wir* ("we") was not used at this point as it had been in the previous sentences.

[8] *Der rote Kampfflieger* (1917), pp.39–40; *The Red Baron*, pp.18–19.

Right: A photo and message provided by the Royal Air Force that informed the German *Luftstreitkräfte* of Richthofen's fate.

To,—
        The German Flying Corps.

Rittmeister Baron MANFRIED von RICHTOFEN

was   killed   in   aerial combat

on   April   21st.   1917.

He   was   buried   with   full

military   honours.

                      From British Royal Air Force.

Es starb für König und Vaterland unser heiß-
geliebter ältester Sohn und Bruder

Rittmeister

Manfred Freiherr von Richthofen
(Ulan 1),

Ritter des hohen Ordens „pour le mérite"
und höchster Orden,
Kommandeur eines Jagdgeschwaders,
im noch nicht vollendeten 26. Lebensjahre.

In tiefer stolzer Trauer
Albrecht Freiherr von Richthofen,
Major, z. D. im Felde.
Kunigunde Freifrau von Richthofen,
geb. v. Schickfus u. Neudorff.
Ilse Freiin von Richthofen.
Lothar Freiherr von Richthofen (Drag. 4),
Ritter des hohen Ordens „pour le mérite",
Leutnant und Führer einer Jagdstaffel.
Karl Bolko Freiherr von Richthofen,
Kadett.

Schweidnitz, im April 1918.   1105/10

Above: The death announcement issued by the Richthofen family. It said: "He died for king and country, our dearly beloved son and brother *Rittmeister* Manfred *Freiherr* von Richthofen, (1st Uhlans), knight of the high *Pour le Mérite* order and the highest orders, commander of a *Jagdgeschwader*, who had still not completed 26 years of life. In deep, proud mourning: Albrecht *Freiherr* von Richthofen, Major (retired) in the field; Kunigunde *Freifrau* von Richthofen, neé von Schickfus und Neudorff; Ilse *Freiin* von Richthofen; Lothar *Freiherr* von Richthofen (4th Dragoons), knight of the high *Pour le Mérite* order, *Leutnant* and *Jagdstaffel* CO; Karl Bolko *Freiherr* von Richthofen, cadet. Schweidnitz, April 1918."

[9] Richthofen only dictated his memoirs and someone else undoubtedly edited them into their final form. What is not known is the extent to which his dictations were amended or supplemented. The book was undoubtedly issued for propaganda reasons and may have been heavily influenced to that end.

[10] *Der rote Kampfflieger* (1917), p.28; *The Red Baron*, p.11.

[11] *Der rote Kampfflieger* (1917), p.41; *The Red Baron*, p.20.

[12] *Richthofen, Ein Heldenleben* (Berlin:Verlag Ullstein, 1920), p.182; *The Red Baron*, p.23.

[13] *Mein Kriegstagebuch*, p.57; *Mother of Eagles*, p.83.

[14] *Der rote Kampfflieger* (1917), pp.45–46; *The Red Baron*, pp.24–25.

[15] *Der rote Kampfflieger* (1917), p.49; *The Red Baron*, p.27.

[16] *Der rote Kampfflieger* (1917), p.55; *The Red Baron*, p.31.

[17] *Der rote Kampfflieger* (1917), p.61; *The Red Baron*, p.34.

[18] *Der rote Kampfflieger* (1917), p.59; *The Red Baron*, p.33.

[19] *Der rote Kampfflieger* (1917), p.63; *The Red Baron*, p.36.

[20] *Der rote Kampfflieger* (1917), pp.63–64; *The Red Baron*, p.36.

[21] *Der rote Kampfflieger* (1917), pp.65–66; *The Red*

Right: Richthofen's coffin is carried from Berlin's *Gnadenkirche* (in *Invalidenpark* before being razed in 1967) before being placed on a gun carriage for transport to the city's Invalidenfriedhof cemetery. The pallbearers and honor guard were all *Pour le Mérite* airmen. Standing beneath the saluting soldiers to the left, in full profile, is Otto Könnecke with Carl Degelow, Alfred Keller, and Franz Walz to the right from him. To the right of the coffin (left to right): Julius Buckler, Karl Bolle (obscured by Buckler), Heinrich Bongartz, Curt Wüsthoff.

Above: A group portrait of the *Pour le Mérite* airmen who attended Richthofen's reinterment ceremony in Berlin on 20 November 1925. Left to right: Bruno Loerzer, Franz Walz, Julius Buckler, Paul Bäumer, Hermann Köhl, Alfred Keller, Josef Mai, Theo Osterkamp, Otto Könnecke, Josef Veltjens, Josef Jacobs, Heinrich Bongartz, Arthur Laumann, Gotthard Sachsenberg, Leo Leonhardy, Karl Bolle, Hans Klein, Oskar von Boenigk, Carl Degelow, Curt Wüsthoff.

48

Above: Richthofen's original grave marker at Invalidenfriedhof. The Nazis eventually replaced it with a more substantial monument.

Baron, p.36–37.

[22] This seems to have alluded to the banged-up condition in which training machines often ended.

[23] *Der rote Kampfflieger* (1917), pp.67–68; *The Red Baron*, p.38.

[24] *Mein Kriegstagebuch*, pp.68–69; *Mother of Eagles*, p.90. The fact that this took place on Christmas Eve rather than Christmas day was later specified by *Freifrau* von Richthofen at the end of her diary entry: "This Christmas Eve, which I was allowed to spend under the Christmas tree with all my children and my husband, made me feel grateful and happy."

[25] *Der rote Kampfflieger* (1917), pp.72–73; *The Red Baron*, p.41.

[26] *Der rote Kampfflieger* (1917), p.75; *The Red Baron*, p.43.

[27] *Ein Heldenleben*, p.189; *The Red Baron*, p.46.

[28] See Peter Supf, *Das Buch der deutschen Fluggeschichte* Vol.II, p.437.

[29] *Ein Heldenleben*, p.190; *The Red Baron*, p.48.

[30] *Der rote Kampfflieger* (1917), pp.88–89; *The Red Baron*, pp.52–53. Either Richthofen or his ghost writer exaggerated somewhat about having ridden straight across Germany to his new assignment after his departure from Kowel on 18 August. Richthofen did not arrive at *Jasta* 2 until 1 September and his mother related that this was because he had stopped home first on 25 August and hunted for awhile with his father.

[31] Boelcke had single victories on 2, 8, and 9 September and double victories on 14 and 15 September.

[32] *Der rote Kampfflieger* (1917), pp.90–93; *The Red Baron*, pp.53–55. Interestingly, the custom of placing a stone on a grave as proof of visitation and respect for the dead is normally associated with the Jewish faith. Morris was buried in the Porte-de-Paris Cemetery just outside of Cambrai whereas Rees was interred in the Plouich Communal Cemetery close to where their plane

Above: The Richthofen family plot in Wiesbaden's Südfriedhof cemetery. Directly in front of the Baroness' headstone is daughter Ilse's plaque and then son Manfred's marker. Bolko's plaque is to the right of them, and to the left (here mostly obscured by greenery) is Lothar's "in memorium" marker.

fell (Villers Plouich).

[33] Rees was promoted to Captain on the day of his death, so some sources list him with that rank.

[34] In a bizarre and terrible twist of fate, Rees' brother, John, was killed the very same day when he was struck by lightning.

[35] *Mein Kriegstagebuch*, p.86; *Mother of Eagles*, p.105. For more on this accident, see *Blue Max Airmen* Vol.1, pp.26–28.

[36] *Ein Heldenleben*, p.330.

[37] Richthofen said Hawker attacked him from above (*Der rote Kampfflieger* 1917, p.103; *The Red Baron*, p.61) whereas the official British communiqué indicated it was Richthofen who dove on Hawker (Cole, *Royal Flying Corps 1915–1916*, p.323).

[38] *Der rote Kampfflieger* (1917), pp.103–05; *The Red Baron*, pp.61–62.

[39] *Der rote Kampfflieger* (1917), pp.106–07; *The Red Baron*, p.63.

[40] *Ein Heldenleben*, p.194; *The Red Baron*, p.64.

[41] Ibid.

[42] Though the bracing helped, the problem continued to plague the type until further modifications were made to fighters delivered to the front that summer.

[43] *Mein Kriegstagebuch*, pp.96–97; *Mother of Eagles*, p.115.

[44] *Der rote Kampfflieger* (1917), p.108; *The Red Baron*, p.64.

[45] *Ein Heldenleben*, p.206.

[46] *Jasta* 11's other victors: *Lt.* Karl-Emil Schaefer (7); *Lt.* Carl Allmenröder (5); *Lt.* Kurt Wolff (5); *Vzfw.* Sebastian Festner (2); *Lt.* Constantin Krefft (1); *Lt.* Lothar von Richthofen (1).

[47] *Mein Kriegstagebuch*, pp.105–06; *Mother of Eagles*, p.121.

[48] This appears to have occurred during the period of 20–26 April 1917. See Bronnenkant, *The Imperial German Eagles* Vol.1, pp.331–37.

[49] *Ein Heldenleben*, p.143.

[50] *Mein Kriegstagebuch*, pp.108–09; *Mother of Eagles*, pp.122–24.

[51] *Der rote Kampfflieger* (1917), p.162; *The Red Baron*, p.96.

[52] *Mein Kriegstagebuch*, p.113; *Mother of Eagles*,

p.126.

[53] The reverse of photos of Richthofen's departure from Krefeld give the date as 13 June 1917.

[54] *Mein Kriegstagebuch*, p.115; *Mother of Eagles*, p.129.

[55] Allmenröder's death has been variously attributed to Raymond Collishaw or ground fire; see Bronnenkant, *The Imperial German Eagles* Vol. 1, pp.318–19.

[56] *Mein Kriegstagebuch*, pp.124–25; *Mother of Eagles*, p.136.

[57] Quoted in a clipping from an unidentified 1934 newspaper on file in Stadtarchiv Solingen.

[58] *Ein Heldenleben*, p.148.

[59] Ibid., pp.149–50.

[60] Kraske's photo album dedicated to Richthofen was recently sold on auction.

[61] Bodenschatz, *Jagd in Flanderns Himmel*, p.33; *Hunting with Richthofen*, p.29.

[62] *Jagd in Flanderns Himmel*, p.40; *Hunting with Richthofen*, p.35.

[63] *Der rote Kampfflieger* (1933), p.149; *The Red Baron*, p.111.

[64] *Jagd in Flanderns Himmel*, p.37; *Hunting with Richthofen*, p.32.

[65] *Jagd in Flanderns Himmel*, p.43; *Hunting with Richthofen*, p.38.

[66] Those scenes are part of two reels taken by Fokker that can be viewed on the United States Holocaust Memorial Museum's website at http://www.ushmm.org/search/results/?q=fokker.

[67] *Jagd in Flanderns Himmel*, p.44; *Hunting with Richthofen*, p.38.

[68] Richthofen's mother stated that the plane was her son's "*Privateigentum*" or "private property" (see *Mein Kriegstagebuch*, p.127; *Mother of Eagles*, p.138). This may or may not have been technically true; in either case, other photos demonstrate it was used by other men in the unit.

[69] *Jagd in Flanderns Himmel*, p.45; *Hunting with Richthofen*, p.40.

[70] One line stated: "With his friendly nature and quiet modesty, he was one of the dearest and best comrades to us all."

[71] His mother's diary said he returned to Schweidnitz on 17 September and 9 October. Richthofen's 30 September letter to her from Gotha indicates that he was still at the duke's estate at that point (see *Mein Kriegstagebuch*, p.127; *Mother of Eagles*, p.138 and *Ein Heldenleben*, p.199). He went on to state that he was leaving for Berlin that day and would be in Schweidnitz about a week after that. When *Freifrau* von Richthofen spoke of the news of the deaths of Wolff and Voss, she made no mention of Manfred's reaction or presence, though she did speak of Lothar's; so it does not appear that Manfred was in Schweidnitz in mid-September and that the 17 September date was in error.

[72] They were Lübeck's Hanseatic Cross on 22 September, Brusnwick's War Merit Cross, 2nd Class on 24 September, Hamburg's Hanseatic Cross on 25 September, Schaumburg-Lippe's Cross for Faithful Service, 2nd Class on 10 October, and Lippe's War Honor Cross for Heroic Act on 13 October.

[73] *Mein Kriegstagebuch*, p.129; *Mother of Eagles*, p.139.

[74] Johannes Werner, *Briefe eines deutschen Kampffliegers an ein junges Mädchen*, pp.202–03.

[75] *Ein Heldenleben*, pp.159–60.

[76] Georg von der Osten, "Memoirs of World War I with Jagdstaffeln 11 and 4," *C&C* 15:3, p.224. Lothar von Richthofen told the same anecdote this way: "A gentleman stood by the picture. He went up to him and said: 'Don't you think the picture bears a certain resemblance to me?' The gentleman turned around, looked my brother up and down with astonishment and said: 'No, you shouldn't get any big ideas about that.'" (*Ein Heldenleben*, p.224)

[77] *Der rote Kampfflieger* (1933), pp.203–04.

[78] *Mein Kriegstagebuch*, pp.150–51; *Mother of Eagles*, p.157.

[79] Ibid.

[80] *Mein Kriegstagebuch*, p.152; *Mother of Eagles*, p.157.

[81] *Ein Heldenleben*, p.260.

[82] *Richthofen-Flieger*, pp.22–23. Karl Bodenschatz, probably borrowing from Wenzl, related the same anecdote in *Jagd in Flanderns Himmel*, p.80; *Hunting with Richthofen*, p.73.

[83] A film of the ceremony and other related scenes can be viewed at http://www.ww1westernfront.gov.au/villers-bretonneux/amiens-cathedral/von-richthofens-funeral-movie.php.

[84] His former plot no.1177 is now marked as the grave of Sebastian Paustian.

[85] Three additional *Pour le Mérite* award winners – Josef Jacobs, Theo Osterkamp and Gotthard Sachsenberg – attended the ceremony as well. See Bronnenkant, *Imperial German Eagles* Vol.3, pp.175–84 for a description and many photos of the event.

[86] Ilse's husband, Nicol von Reibnitz (died 30 December 1968), is buried with her. Lothar was interred alongside father Albrecht (†1920) in Schweidnitz and their graves are now unmarked.

Facing Page: This image, created by RFC/RAF war artist Joseph Simpson, appeared on the front of RAF No.209 Squadron's 1918 Christmas card. Note the use of the term "Red Baron."

THE END *of the* RED BARON

Manfred von Richthofen – The Aircraft

Just as with Richthofen's life and career, numerous studies and profiles have already been performed on the aircraft he flew.[1] What follows is a synopsis of those efforts, supplemented by some updated information (including some new aircraft identifications for Richthofen) and several previously unpublished photos. The aircraft reviewed below are those we know or believe he flew in either as an observer before he earned his pilot's license or as a pilot. The aircraft in which he was "chauffeured" behind the lines by other pilots at the controls (e.g., during his May–June 1917 leave) are not included. Though the list below is extensive, it is highly likely that Richthofen also flew aircraft other than those discussed here.

Unknown Biplanes (as an observer)
(Late May—20 August 1915)
Richthofen went home to Schweidnitz on 21 May 1915 and announced to his mother that he was joining the Air Service. He departed on 25 May to be evaluated as an observer at *FEA* 7.[2] Richthofen was selected for further training and sent to *FEA* 6 on 10 June. An assignment in the field with *FFA 69* followed on 21 June, where he remained until his transfer to *B.A.O.* on 21 August. It is believed that *FEA* 7 and 6 employed Aviatik and Kondor aircraft, respectively, at the time; but we have no specific information regarding the machines Richthofen manned as an observer during this period other than this vague statement in one of his letters quoted in the 1933 version of his autobiography: "There is a *riesiger Apparat* [giant apparatus] at *Flieger-Ersatz-Abteilung* 7 for us to train in."[3]

AEG G.II (possibly G.6/15), Unknown Biplane (as an observer)
(21 August—Early November 1915)
Richthofen stated he was "transferred to a *Grosskampfflugzeug* [large combat plane]" at *Brieftauben-Abteilung Ostende* on 21 August.[4] We know from unit records that this was the AEG G.II, which, by virtue of its being armed with two or three machine guns, was designated as a "large combat plane" even though it could also be used as a bomber. Though it could carry a crew of three, Richthofen's writings indicate that it was sometimes manned by only two men. It was in this type that Richthofen shed his "first drop of blood for the Fatherland" on 4 September when the little finger of his right hand was smacked by one of his machine's propellers. The late air historian A.E. Ferko identified Richthofen's G.II as G.6/15 (see MvR1 below) but the exact provenance of that information was left unexplained.[5] Richthofen was in a biplane "somewhat smaller than our old barge" with Paul Henning von Osterroht as pilot when he claimed his first, though unconfirmed, victory. The precise type is unknown.

MvR1: This photo displays AEG G.II G.6/15. The late A.E. Ferko claimed that this was the plane in which Richthofen and Georg Zeumer often flew together.

1. AEG G.II G.6/15

Unknown Biplanes (as a pilot)
(Early October 1915—15 March 1916)
After meeting and speaking with *Lt.* Oswald Boelcke on a train taking them both to their new assignment at Rethel in early October 1915, Richthofen resolved to become a pilot. Georg Zeumer tutored him and sent him off on his first solo flight – which turned out to be unsuccessful – on 10 October. Richthofen continued his pilot training at *FEA* 2 in November and passed his final pilot's examination on Christmas Day. His first assignment in the field as a pilot came when he arrived at *Kagohl* 2's *Kasta* 8 on 16 March 1916. The types of biplanes he flew during this period are unknown.

Zeppelin-Staaken V.G.O.III or R.IV? (as an observer)
(Early November 1915)
On 2 November 1915, Richthofen wrote: "I have been ordered to [fly in] a *Riesenflugzeug* [giant airplane] but it unfortunately isn't ready yet. Therefore, my pilot, a *Herr* von Osterroht, and I must go to Berlin in the near future to become acquainted with the giant barge... Five to six men fly in it: a mechanic, machine gunner, two pilots, an observer."[6] More than one source has suggested it was one of Siemens-Schuckert's Steffen R series aircraft, but that type was manned by no more than four crewmen. It seems more likely that Richthofen was referring to one of the early Zeppelin-Staaken "giants" that carried a larger complement – possibly the V.G.O. (*Versuchs Gotha Ost*) III or the R.IV.[7] Having said that, though Osterroht and Richthofen did travel to Berlin, we cannot be sure that Richthofen ever actually flew in a *Riesenflugzeug* because he went to *FEA* 2 for pilot training at Döberitz shortly afterwards on 15 November.

LVG C.II, LFG Roland C.II (as a pilot)
(16 March—End of June 1916)
Photographic evidence confirms that *Kasta* 8, where Richthofen arrived on 16 March 1916, flew both the LVG C.II and LFG Roland C.II *Walfisch* at Mont before its move to the Eastern Front at the end of June.[8] If Ferko's assertion that the *Walfisch* arrived at *Kasta* 8 "in about May 1916" is correct, then Richthofen would have flown both types.[9] Years ago, based upon a poorer copy of MvR2 than is presented below, it was speculated that one of the men sitting atop the *Walfisch* marked with black spheres resembled Richthofen and that he may have flown that plane. Magnification of MvR2 rules this out. Intriguingly, however, Richthofen may still have been in the photograph. Someone resembling him is sitting on the *Walfisch* marked with an "X" at far left, and next to him is someone who looks like Alfred Gerstenberg; but the evidence is inconclusive and cannot be taken as proof that Richthofen flew the "X" plane.

MvR2: A lineup of *Kasta* 8's LFG Roland C.II *Walfisch* aircraft at Mont. Closer examination (see blowup) of the two men sitting atop the one marked with black circles demonstrates that neither of them was Richthofen, as was previously speculated. A closeup of the the plane marked with an "X" at far left, however, displays two men who look similar to Richthofen (left) and Alfred Gerstenberg (right). Nevertheless, this identification is by no means positive. (photo courtesy of Greg VanWyngarden)

2. LFG Roland C.II possibly flown by MvR

Fokker E.III
(May—End of June 1916)

On 3 May 1916, Richthofen wrote that he was "flying a Fokker, which is the airplane with which Boelcke and Immelmann have been tremendously successful."[10] He had gone to the *Armee-Flug-Park* at Montmédy for single-seat fighter training in late March 1916 and upon his return was allowed to share an *Eindecker* with *Lt.* Hans Reimann. After Reimann was forced to destroy that plane following an emergency landing in no-man's-land, Richthofen obtained another *Eindecker* only to crash and demolish it in late June. MvR3 and 4 are photos of the wreck that reveal that it was an E.III model.[11] Given the time period, this was probably true for the plane he and Reimann had shared as well.

MvR3–4: Two of several photos taken of the Fokker E.III in which Richthofen crashed in late June 1915. The second image includes his dog, Moritz. (second photo courtesy of Jim Miller)

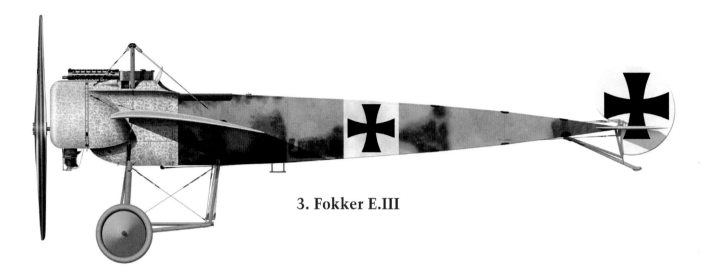

3. Fokker E.III

Albatros Biplane
(Summer 1916)

Richthofen described an incident in the "summer of 1916" (but before *Kasta* 8's move to the Eastern Front on 28 June) where he flew "my good Albatros" through a thunderstorm.[12] The model is unknown.

Albatros C.III, Rumpler C.I
(1 July—Late August 1916)

Richthofen provided no details on the type of plane(s) he flew after *Kasta* 8 arrived at Kowel on 1 July 1916. A photograph taken of him at Kowel (see O'Connor, *Aviation Awards of Imperial Germany in World War I* Vol.5, p.322) has a number of Albatros C.III aircraft and one Rumpler C.I in the background. It does not appear that he did any *Eindecker* flying during this period.

Fokker D.I, Halberstadt D-type fighter?
(1–15 September 1916)

When Richthofen arrived at *Jasta* 2's Vélu airfield on 1 September 1916, the unit had only a Fokker D.I, a Fokker D.III, a Halberstadt fighter, and an Albatros D.I at its disposal. If Richthofen did any practice flying during this period, it likely would have been in one or both of the Fokker D.I and Halberstadt fighters because (i) his CO, Oswald Boelcke, usually flew the Fokker D.III, and (ii) Richthofen wrote on 18 September: "I've recently flown a backup machine with which I haven't been able to do much and have usually come up short in air combat," a comment that does not seem to suit the Albatros D.I.[13]

Albatros D.I 381/16 or 391/16
(16 September—November 1916?)

Boelcke, Richthofen, and several other *Jasta* 2 pilots collected six new Albatros fighters from *AFP* 1 on 16 September 1916 – a D.II for Boelcke and five D.Is for his men. Richthofen stated that he took his assigned plane up and gained his first official victory in it the next day. MvR5 is a recently discovered photo that probably shows that machine. It bears the same white stripe on its nose that appears on what is presumed to have been Richthofen's later Albatros D.II (see below). Lothar von Richthofen stated that when his brother was still with *Jasta* Boelcke, he had experimented with painting his plane with "*anderem erdfarben*" ("various earth colors") to try to make it less visible when approaching an opponent in the air (see above, p.20). Note that almost the entire fuselage of this airplane appears to have been overpainted, leaving only a small, rectangular patch around the fin's serial number and the metal panel just aft of the spinner untouched.[14] Under magnification, the serial number is 3?1/16, with the "?" possibly being 0, 3, 6, 8 or 9. As far as we know, there were no Albatros D.I aircraft numbered 301, 331 or 361, which leaves either 381 or 391. We have photos of 391/16 – a *Jasta* Boelcke plane piloted by *Lt.* Karl Heinrich Büttner – just after its capture by the British on 16 November 1916 and it does not have a white stripe on its nose. Still, parts of the machine had been repainted (e.g., Büttner's personal "Bü" insignia had been added and the tail fin's serial number overpainted), so it is possible that the nose stripe had been covered over.

One final note on this aircraft: one of the pilots involved in the 16 October 1916 fight in which Richthofen achieved his fifth victory, 2Lt. C.G. Baker, reported that he saw "a red-doped aircraft (Nieuport type) and two Rolands" during the struggle.[15] This is too early to have been Richthofen's "*Le Petit Rouge*," but we might speculate that it nevertheless was Richthofen flying

MvR5

MvR5: A hitherto unpublished photo of a lineup of *Jasta* Boelcke Albatros D.Is at Lagnicourt airfield. The closeup features the Albatros D.I, serial number 381/16 or 391/16, that may have been flown by Richthofen during his first few months as a fighter pilot. *Lt.* Jürgen Sandel's D.I 431/16, marked with an "S" on the fuselage, is second from the left. *Lt.* Otto Höhne's D.I 390/16, similarly marked with "Hö," is third from the right. At far right is D.I 427/16, pilot unknown.

MvR5-Blowup

4a. Albatros D.I D.381/16

in this or another machine that had been painted a reddish brown – an earth color already in use on German aircraft.

Richthofen may have flown his D.I until sometime in November when he evidently upgraded to a D.II.

4b. Albatros D.I D.391/16

Albatros D.II 481/16

(November 1916?—6 January 1917)

MvR6–8 show Richthofen in the vicinity of an Albatros D.II with a white spinner and a white stripe around its nose, and it therefore seems likely that it was his personal mount. MvR9–12 are four hitherto unpublished photos of the same D.II fighter at Lagnicourt airfield. Richthofen mentioned his D.II's serial number – "D.481"– in the combat report for his 15th victory, shot down on 27 December 1916.[16] This may or may not have been the D.II pictured here in MvR6–12. In any event, MvR7 shows Richthofen in company with *Lt.* Hans Wortmann,

who arrived at *Jasta* Boelcke in early November 1916, and *Oblt.* Stefan Kirmaier, who was killed in action on 22 November; so it appears that he had switched to a D.II by that time. The Albatros fighter in MvR6–12 shows signs of having been overpainted, just like the D.I above. Presumably, its fuselage was covered with one or more of the earth colors mentioned by Lothar von Richthofen.

The new Albatros D.III model began to be delivered to frontline units in January 1917. *Jasta* Boelcke received its first shipment of them on 7 January, and Richthofen probably switched over to one almost immediately.

MvR8

MvR6: Richthofen poses in front of what was presumably his Albatros D.II, marked with a white spinner and white stripe around its nose.

MvR7: A smiling and casually-dressed Richthofen poses again in front of the same plane with three of his *Jasta* Boelcke comrades. Left to right: *Oblt.* Stefan Kirmaier (CO), *Lt.* Hans Imelmann, Richthofen, *Lt.* Hans Wortmann. The

photo was taken at Lagnicourt airfield in November 1916.

MvR8: This photo, taken the same time as MvR7, offers a broader view of *Jasta* Boelcke's lineup that day. At left is Richthofen's alleged D.II, followed by three D.I models. The group of men in the foreground with their backs to the camera are (left to right): Richthofen, Imelmann, and Wortmann.

MvR9

MvR9-Blowup

5. Albatros D.II D.481/16

MvR10

MvR10-Blowup

MvR9–12: Four previously unpublished photos of Richthofen's probable D.II at Lagnicourt airfield. The first captures it getting ready to take off. The second shows it at far left in company with two Albatros D.Is. In the third image, its tail has been lifted onto a wooden support while *Lt.* Jürgen Sandel's S-marked D.I 431/16 rests at left. The final picture shows the machine on the left end of a *Kette* ("chain" or small flight) of D.I aircraft that included *Lt.* Hans Wortmann's 434/16 (marked with a "W") at far right.

MvR11-Blowup

MvR11

MvR12

MvR12-Blowup

Albatros D.III *"Le Petit Rouge"*
(7?–24 January 1917)

Richthofen noted in his combat report dated 24 January 1917 (victory 18) that he was flying an "Albatros D.III" when he was forced to make an emergency landing because of a cracked wing. He also commented that according to his English victims (who were taken prisoner), "my red painted plane was not unknown to them, as when being asked who had brought them down they answered, '*Le petit Rouge.*'"[17] There is little doubt then that Richthofen had had his D.III painted predominantly red by this point. What still eludes us, however, is the precise timing of when that occurred. If he had adopted a red color scheme upon his arrival at *Jasta* 11, that would have given *"Le Petit Rouge"* only a little more than a day to have become known by his opponents at the front. Though it is not impossible that the news of such a garishly painted plane spread that swiftly, the timeframe still seems problematically short. It is therefore possible that he had had his D.III painted red soon after its arrival at

Jasta Boelcke. As was noted earlier, *Jasta* Boelcke's base at Pronville was only about 20 kilometers south of *Jasta* 11's La Brayelle airfield, and word of *"Le Petit Rouge"* could easily have spread among the British units facing them both along this close front. Whatever the exact case, we can at least point to January 1917 as the birth month of *der rote Kampfflieger*.

The serial number of *"Le Petit Rouge"* has eluded historians for years. A.E. Ferko listed four Albatros D.III fighters as having been sent to *Jasta* 11 on 21 and 22 January.[18] According to Richthofen, his first day with *Jasta* 11 followed on 22–23 January (see page 19 above), so it is possible that one of them had been intended for him. They were 1993/16 and 1996/16 on 21 January and 1960/16 and 1991/16 on 22 January. Ferko also noted their eventual disposition, stating that 1993/16 was scrapped and sent to Adlershof on 13 April 1917, 1996/16 went to Treptow on 11 May 1917, 1960/16 was given to a *Jastaschule* (fighter pilot school) on 17 September 1917, and 1991/16 was damaged on 24 May 1917. We can rule out (i) 1993/16 because Richthofen was still flying *"Le Petit Rouge"* after 13 April, (ii) 1996/16 because it may have been *Lt.* Hans-Georg Eduard Lübbert's mount and was later used for aerial photographic missions (see below, p.70), and (iii) 1960/16 because it is highly doubtful that such a famous (and worn-out) aircraft would have been used at a fighter school. This leaves us with 1991/16, which was damaged on 24 May (and presumably scrapped thereafter) while Richthofen was away on leave, as a possible candidate.

Other historians have surmised that Richthofen had been allowed to bring his *Jasta* Boelcke D.III with him to *Jasta* 11 – their airfields at Pronville and La Brayelle were only 20 kilometers or so apart. Unfortunately, the serial number of his *Jasta* Boelcke D.III remains unknown.[19]

Several other Albatros D.IIIs experienced wing failure around the same time as Richthofen's. As a result, the type was subsequently grounded on 27 January pending an investigation into the cause. Prior to his arrival, *Jasta* 11 had been equipped with several Halberstadt D.V fighters and Richthofen temporarily switched over to at least one of them.

Halberstadt D.V

(25 January–Early March? 1917)
Richthofen's combat report for his next victory on 1 February noted: "I managed to approach him within 50 yards apparently unnoticed, with my Halberstaedter machine."[20] If the identification of RFC No.2 Squadron's BE.2c 2543 as Richthofen's 14 February victory is correct, then it appears he was flying a Halberstadt then too, because the hostile aircraft that attacked it were described in the unit's combat report as "three Halberstadt Scouts."[21] Whether or not he used a Halberstadt after that is a matter of debate because Richthofen never disclosed in his combat reports what type of aircraft he flew during March 1917.

Some historians, citing accounts from British airmen who may have confronted Richthofen, contend that he continued flying a Halberstadt throughout March. The first such example involves Richthofen's 22nd victory, brought down on 4 March. It is said that his probable victim reported being attacked by "a single-seat Halberstadt Scout with multi-coloured wings."[22] This could have been Richthofen in a Halberstadt, many of which bore red/brown and olive green patches on the upper surfaces of their wings and light blue underneath. The next example comes from two reports submitted by men who might have been in a fight where Richthofen and *Lt.* Hans-Georg Lübbert were both brought down on 6 March. One

of the reports mentioned "a machine painted mostly green" and the other "a Halberstadt" as having been hit.[23] This does not comply well with what Richthofen and Lübbert had to say about the event, however. When Richthofen recounted the incident in his autobiography, he stated that while he was gliding down to an emergency landing near Hénin Liétard, he watched another plane fall out of the fight: *"Auch ein Albatros"* ("An Albatros too"). Further confirmation of the type is found in his earlier statements: *"ich...gebe einige Probeschüsse, die Gewehre sind in Ordnung"* ("I...fire off a few shots, the guns are in order) and *"Vor sich hat man einen über einhundertundfünfzig 'Pferde' starken Explosionsmotor"* ("Up front there is an internal combustion engine over 150 'horses' strong").[24] The Halberstadt D.V had only one gun and a 120 hp engine whereas the Albatros D.III indeed had two machine guns and a 160 hp engine.

Lübbert was the man flying the other Albatros that Richthofen had observed going down. He had been wounded by a grazing shot to the chest and managed to touch down safely near Richthofen. Richthofen mentioned that there had been four other men in his flight, and Lübbert related the following color schemes for them in his flight log entry for 6 March:

"Obltn. Freiherr von Richthofen
    Bright Red
Ltn. Carl Emil Schäfer
    Yellow with Black Tail
Ltn. Kurt Wolff
    Plum Purple
Ltn. Carl Allmenröder
    Field Gray
Ltn. Edy Lübbert
    Half Blue, Half Yellow"[25]

There is ample photographic evidence to confirm that these color schemes were indeed applied to their Albatros fighters. So it does not appear that either Richthofen or Lübbert were in the "machine painted mostly green" or the "Halberstadt" (unless an Albatros had been mistaken for this type, which did sometimes occur).

After his emergency landing on 6 March, Richthofen said he had lunch at a nearby ground unit and then flew Lübbert's machine back to La Brayelle because his had been incapacitated by shots through its engine and fuel tanks. Later that same evening, around 5:00 p.m., Richthofen shot down his 24th victim – RFC No.16 Squadron's BE.2e A2785. Another 16 Squadron crew related that they watched their comrades spin down and then encountered "a white-coloured machine" as well as a "bright red

Halberstadt."[26] We might have considered "bright red Halberstadt" to have been a mistake for "bright red Albatros" except that Richthofen had left what Lübbert identified as his red Albatros on the ground near Hénin Liétard. The damage it had suffered almost certainly kept it out of action for at least the remainder of the day. So did Richthofen really take up a red Halberstadt that evening? That would have been strange, because we know Richthofen was no fan of the Halberstadt D.V. In *Oberstlt.* Wilhelm Siegert's discussion of a meeting that had been convened in Cambrai on 22 December 1916 to discuss the future development of fighter aircraft, he noted that among all the pilots in attendance, only Richthofen had been a strong advocate of the 160 hp Albatros over the 120 hp Halberstadt D.V.[27] The 27 January 1917 grounding of the Albatros D.III model was rescinded on 19 February after wing reinforcement modifications by the manufacturer had been tested, found satisfactory, and made available to frontline units. It seems likely then, that once those modifications had been made to *"Le Petit Rouge,"* he would have immediately gone back to using it – which he appears to have done by 6 March at the latest. Records show that *Jasta* 11 received no less than six, and possibly as many as eight, more Albatros D.IIIs during the period 25–27 February, so one would think *"Le Petit Rouge"* could also have been available by then.[28] Furthermore, since Richthofen had retrieved Lübbert's machine and flown it back to La Brayelle on 6 March, why would he have flown what he considered to have been an inferior Halberstadt later that same day when Lübbert's, or any other *Jasta* 11 pilot's, Albatros mount would have been available to him. Richthofen indeed did just that when he borrowed the recovering Lübbert's half-blue, half-yellow plane to bring down his 27th victory on 17 March.[29] As it turns out, we otherwise would have known that Richthofen was not flying a Halberstadt during that engagement because his combat report stated he downed his opponent "after 800 shots."[30] The Halberstadt D.V carried only 500 rounds while the Albatros was armed with 1,000.[31]

Upon review, it appears that Richthofen returned to flying *"Le Petit Rouge"* on or before 6 March, at which point it was temporarily put out of action. After that he could have turned to a Halberstadt D.V (which may or may not have been painted red) again. His preference for the Albatros D.III, however, probably made that a rare occurrence and it is more likely that he flew a D.III whenever possible during the remainder of March (see below). Records show that he had his choice of several that remained on hand at *Jasta* 11 in February and March.[32]

Albatros D.III 2006/16 (with red band around fuselage) (Intermittently, March–April 1917)

Lothar von Richthofen related the following in 1920:

"When I came as a total beginner to my brother's *Staffel*, he gave me one of his old machines with which he had achieved 10 air victories. He also gave me a pair of old, worn fur gloves... As luck would have it, I shot down my first 10 Englishmen armed with those gloves and that machine. Following those 10 victories, our crate – the one that had a red band around the fuselage – was so shot up that the good old steel horse had to be transported back home. Manfred also stayed extraordinarily [long] with his famous red bird. He shot down his 19th–52nd opponents with that machine."[33]

As interesting as this passage may be, it presents a multitude of problems. Lothar reported to *Jasta* 11 on 6 March 1917, at which point his brother Manfred had a total of 24 victories. Only eight of them, however, had been gained with *Jasta* 11. Furthermore, the first two of those eight had been with *"Le Petit Rouge"* followed by at least another three using a Halberstadt D.V. So Manfred could only have begun using the red-banded Albatros D.III as of his 22nd victory on 4 March; but he downed only three aircraft between 4 March and his brother's arrival two days later, which leaves us nowhere near the 10 Lothar had asserted. In order to reach that total, we would have to assume that Lothar had been given Manfred's former red-banded machine just prior to the date of Lothar's first victory, 28 March, and that Manfred had achieved his 22nd (4 March) through 31st (25 March) victories exclusively in that red-banded machine. We know this was not true, however, and even Lothar contradicts it by saying that Manfred had gained victories 19–52 in "his famous red bird." To complicate matters further, Lothar's contradictory statement is also untrue. Manfred's victories 19–21, and 22, occurred in a Halberstadt while victory 27 was achieved with Hans-Georg Eduard Lübbert's half-blue, half-yellow Albatros. So no matter how we do the math, Lothar's assertions do not add up. Nevertheless, we have photo MvR13 that shows Lothar in what presumably was that red-banded machine; and it possibly appears again, third from the front, in MvR19.[34] Lothar's mathematical inaccuracies notwithstanding, the red-

MvR13: Lothar von Richthofen sits in a plane marked with a band around its fuselage during a conversation with *Lt.* Karl-Emil Schaefer. It is one of the earlier production models because its radiator is centered in the upper wing. Note the white patch that is in the lower left quadrant of the fuselage cross. It matches that seen on D.III 2006/16 in MvR15 below.

MvR13

MvR14

MvR14–15: Two pictures of Richthofen taking off from La Brayelle airfield sometime between 5 and 13 April 1917. In the first, *Lt.* Karl-Emil Schaefer's D.III 2062/16 is to the left of what was identified as Richthofen's plane, followed by two unidentifiable D.IIIs. Schaefer is the man standing second from the right in the dark overcoat. The second image shows the "Richthofen plane" taking off a few moments later. Under magnification, the aircraft's serial number is clearly seen as "D.2006/16," and the same colored band behind the cockpit and the white patch near the national insignia evident in MvR13 are visible as well.

MvR14-Blowup

MvR15

banded machine seems to have actually existed and he certainly had the impression that it, apart from *"Le Petit Rouge,"* had played an important role in his brother's early career.

We are now able to identify that aircraft for the first time. The reverse of MvR14 bears the notation: *"3 Flugzeuge der Staffel Richthofen beim Start. Richthofen selbst im Flugzeug am weitesten rechts. April 1917 Douai."* ("3 aircraft of the Richthofen Staffel upon takeoff. Richthofen himself in the airplane at far right. April 1917 Douai.") Under magnification, the plane's pilot indeed appears to have been Richthofen (e.g., compare his appearance in MvR16) but the serial number is not legible. MvR15, only recently discovered, shows the man identified as Richthofen taking off in that plane just a few moments after MvR22 had been snapped. A closeup reveals three interesting features: (i) the serial number 2006/16, (ii) a colored band behind the cockpit and (iii) a white patch in the lower left quadrant of the fuselage's national insignia. We know that D.III 2006/16 was delivered to *Jasta* 11 on 24 January 1917, right before the type was grounded. This means it would not have been used until at least 19 February when the flying ban was rescinded. D.III 2006/16 appears in another photo with Richthofen (see page 11 above) where he and *Hptm.* Paul Henning von Osterroht are viewing a map laid out on its lower wing. The

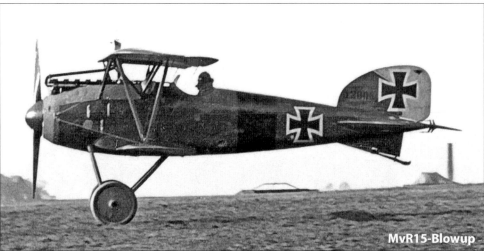

MvR15-Blowup

plane in which Lothar von Richthofen is sitting in MvR13 – the one with a distinct colored band behind the cockpit – displays the exact same white patch near its fuselage cross as seen in MvR15. All of this strongly points to Albatros D.III 2006/16 as the plane with the red band that Lothar said his brother used for some of his early victories before handing it down and switching over to his "famous red bird."

Lothar stated that after he had gained his first 10 victories in his brother's hand-me-down, it "was so shot up that the good old steel horse had to be transported back home." D.III 2006/16 is recorded as having been scrapped on 7 June 1917. If we are correct that it was the red-banded plane used by both Richthofen brothers, then Lothar's math appears to have been faulty once again, because he had achieved not 10 but 24 victories by the time he was wounded and put out of action on 13 May. Still, his assertion that the plane was a wreck at the end of its career agrees with the fact that 2006/16 was indeed scrapped.

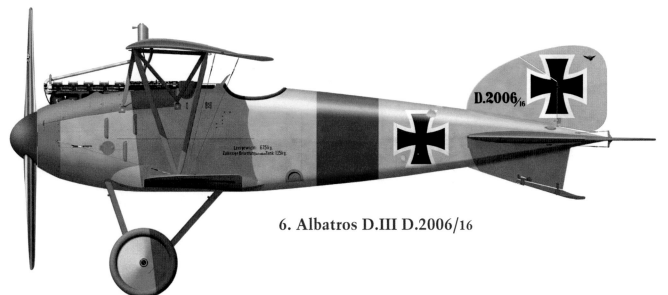

6. Albatros D.III D.2006/16

Albatros D.III *"Le Petit Rouge"*

(Intermittently, early March?—29 April 1917) Richthofen's brother Lothar claimed that Richthofen downed victims 19–52 in his "famous red bird." Though we know that this was not strictly true, Lothar's assertion at least indicates that he believed that his brother had gained many of his late March through April victories with *"Le Petit Rouge."* Numerous photos taken during the closing weeks of April 1917 at *Jasta* 11's airfield outside of Roucourt also attest to the fact that Richthofen was flying *"Le Petit Rouge"* at that time. MvR16–20 are five shots of his mount that tell us that the red paint that covered the entire fuselage obscured its national markings and serial number but left the Albatros logo on the rudder untouched. The wheel covers appear to have been painted red as well, but we cannot be sure if the same was true for the wing surfaces. If they were painted red, their national insignia, or at least those on the upper wing, remained untouched. MvR21 is a rare photo of what almost certainly was *"Le Petit Rouge,"* identified as *"Flugzeug der Oberlt. Freiherr von Richthofen"* ("Airplane of *Oblt. Freiherr* von Richthofen") on its reverse. The reference to Richthofen as an *Oberleutnant* is interesting because he only held that rank from 23 March through 6 April 1917. Accordingly, it was probably an authentic wartime

MvR16: Richthofen takes off in *"Le Petit Rouge."* Most published versions of this image display a later editor's crude attempt to brighten the white border along the fuselage's Maltese Cross. This one, however, faithfully shows how that border, overpainted in red, was only slightly visible.

7. Albatros D.III *Le Petit Rouge*

MvR17: This famous group shot, taken sometime during 20–24 April 1917 at Roucourt, features Richthofen sitting in the cockpit of *"Le Petit Rouge."* The men standing in front of him (left to right): *Lt.* Carl Allmenröder, *Lt.* Hans Hinsch, *Vzfw.* Sebastian Festner, *Lt.* Karl-Emil Schaefer, *Lt.* Kurt Wolff, *Lt.* Georg Simon, *Lt.* Otto Brauneck. Kneeling in front of them are *Lt.* Karl Esser and *Lt.* Constantin Krefft with *Lt.* Lothar von Richthofen sitting on the ground.

identification made around that time with the picture taken beforehand. The airplane bears all the same characteristics as those seen in MvR16–20 (most notably the obscured fuselage insignia yet untouched Albatros logo) except that both it and its paint job appear to be much newer. Note too that the aircraft was in the process of being assembled or disassembled because both sides of the horizontal stabilizer are gone and the cables linking up to the upper wing's ailerons are disconnected. There are no signs of hangars, tents, or other things denoting an airfield location, so we might infer that the picture was taken at the site of an emergency or forced landing and that the plane was being disassembled for transportation elsewhere because it was no longer flightworthy. If this was the case, we know of two such occurrences that involved *"Le Petit Rouge."* The first was Richthofen's emergency

landing on 24 January after his lower wing had cracked. The second was on 6 March 1917 when his fuel tanks and engine were hit and he had to touch down in a meadow near Hénin-Liétard. The odds may favor the latter incident, given its closer proximity to Richthofen's 23 March promotion to *Oberleutnant*. Of course, it is always possible that the photo captured another incident left unmentioned by Richthofen. Either way, this photo clearly demonstrates that the D.III's upper wing insignia were not overpainted and suggests that its upper wing surfaces (at least) may have retained the standard factory finish. Other photos suggest this was the case for *"Le Petit Rouge,"* as does *Lt.* Carl Bauer's diary entry for 15 April: "I also got to meet Richthofen who was there with his half-red Albatros. We called it the 'evening machine.'"[35]

MvR18: Richthofen clambers into the cockpit of "*Le Petit Rouge*." The angle of this shot clearly illustrates that it was an early D.III because its radiator is centrally mounted in the upper wing. Toward the end of the first production run of 400 aircraft, Albatros repositioned the radiator, offsetting it to starboard.

MvR18

MvR19

MvR19: Another famous image taken at Roucourt airfield, with "*Le Petit Rouge*" second from the front. Note that the same bullet-hole patch above and just forward of the over-painted fuselage's national insignia also appears in MvR18.

MvR20

MvR20: A previously unpublished snapshot of the starboard side of *"Le Petit Rouge."* Note the unpainted Albatros logo on the rudder. This image also indicates that the underside of the plane's wings remained in the standard factory finish of light blue.

MvR21

MvR21: A rare image that seems to show *"Le Petit Rouge"* in its early days after an emergency landing. Its condition is decidedly newer than that seen in the images above . Note too that its horizontal stabilizer is missing and that the cables leading to the upper wing ailerons have been disconnected.

Albatros D.III 1996/16?
(17 March 1917)

As mentioned earlier, Richthofen reportedly shot down his 27th victim on 17 March 1917 using Hans-Georg Eduard Lübbert's half-blue, half-yellow Albatros D.III. An Albatros at far right in MvR16 displays a half-and-half color scheme that could have been yellow on top and blue on the bottom (the orthochrome film of the day often reproduced yellow as dark gray or black, and blue as light gray or white). MvR22 is a photo of D.III 1996/16 when it was being flown by a *Lt.* Hohberg of *FF(A)* 263 to take aerial reconnaissance photos, and its appearance

is quite similar to the plane seen in MvR16; note too that someone had painted around the fin's serial number and the rudder's Albatros logo just as was done on other *Jasta* 11 D.IIIs of the time (e.g., Richthofen's *"Le Petit Rouge"* and Karl-Emil Schaefer's 2062/16).[36] Before going to *FF(A)* 263, 1996/16 had served with *Jasta* 11 from 21 January to 11 May 1917, so many believe it is possible that it had been Lübbert's plane. An obvious problem with this identification, however, is that Lübbert was shot down and killed on 30 March 1917. If 1996/16 had been his plane, then what was he brought down in? We may not have the exact answer to that, but we

MvR22

MvR22: Albatros D.III 1996/16 when it was in service with *FA(A)* 263. Note that the Albatros logo on the rudder and a box around the serial number on the tail were not over-painted – a characteristic of some *Jasta* 11 aircraft in March/April 1917. (Photo courtesy of Jim Miller)

MvR23: An Albatros D.III fighter is rolled out of one of *Jasta* 11's hangars hidden in the trees along its Roucourt airfield sometime in late April 1917. At far right is another D.III with a half-and-half color scheme that might have been 1996/16 with the blue and yellow colors reversed on its starboard side.

MvR23

know of multiple instances where a pilot flew one his comrade's mounts and can cite some examples where they were killed in them (e.g., Hans Berr and Paul Hoppe; see Volume 4 of this series, page 98).[37]

So it remains possible that 1996/16 had been Lübbert's half-blue, half-yellow D.III. If so, MvR23 suggests that the color pattern was reversed on the starboard side, with blue on top and yellow below.

8. Albatros D.III D.1996/16

Aviatik C.II
(3 May 1917)

Richthofen wrote that during his visit with *Kaiserin* Auguste Victoria at Bad Homburg vor der Höhe on 3 May, "I had the great pleasure of demonstrating a takeoff for Her Majesty."[38] Richthofen had arrived there in an Aviatik C.II piloted by *Oblt*. Fritz von Falkenhayn and it is presumed that he used that plane for his demonstration for the Empress.

MvR24

MvR24–25: Two of several photographs taken during Richthofen's visit with Empress Auguste Victoria on 3 May. He and Fritz von Falkenhayn had flown there in the Aviatik C.II seen in these images.

MvR25

9. Aviatik C.II

LFG Roland D.III
(Sometime during 16–18 May 1917)

Sometime during the period 16–18 May 1917, Richthofen test flew an LFG Roland D.III at Adlershof airfield outside of Berlin. MvR26–27 show him in that airplane. The type, powered by a 180 hp Argus As.III engine and armed with two machine guns, did not compare favorably with the Albatros line.

MvR26

MvR26–27: Richthofen sits in the cockpit of an LFG Roland D.III fighter at Adlershof field sometime during 16–18 May 1917.

MvR27

10. LFG Roland D.III

Halberstadt Single-Seater
(31 May 1917)

Richthofen's mother recorded in her diary that two men flew from Breslau to Schweidnitz on 31 May to drop off an *"Einsitzer"* ("single-seater") for her son. One of the men who flew on that errand to Schweidnitz was *Lt.* Hans-Georg von der Osten. Many years later, he recalled:

"One day in June [sic] 1917 *Rittmeister Freiherr* von Richthofen landed at Breslau-Gandau and I became acquainted with him. From there, he drove to his family, his mother and sister who were living at Schweidnitz near Breslau. He asked me to fly a plane to him at Schweidnitz as he wished to use it to make some official visits. I did it and thereby also became acquainted with the von Richthofen ladies."[39]

Richthofen was headed for Militsch (now Milicz,

MvR28

MvR28–29: These images were taken while Richthofen was visiting with old comrades. The first shows him in conversation with pre-war friend *Lt.* Alfred Gerstenberg (left). The second has them together with *Hptm.* Viktor Carganico (left of Richthofen), CO of *FEA* 11 near Breslau. There is a Halberstadt D.II behind Richthofen and Gerstenberg in the first image that may or may not have been the "Halberstadt" that Richthofen flew from Schweidnitz to Breslau and then Militsch on 31 May 1917.

Poland) via Breslau. While he was piloting his plane to Breslau, it suddenly flipped over when he momentarliy released the controls. Only his seat belt saved him from being ejected. Then when he tried to fly from Breslau to Militsch, the engine quit.[40] Brother Lothar, relating the same incident, specified that the plane had been a *"Halberstädter Einsitzer"* ("Halberstadt single-seater"). The Baroness further related that it had been *"ein ihm unbekannter Typ"* ("a type unknown to him") whereas Lothar characterized it as a *"ganz fremde Maschine"* ("completely foreign machine").[41] Since we know that Richthofen had flown a Halberstadt D.V before, we can only guess that they meant an earlier model such as the D.II or D.III.

MvR28–29 are two images from a series of photos that captured Richthofen during a visit with his old friend, *Lt.* Alfred Gerstenberg, and their former

Kasta 8 commander, *Hptm.* Viktor Carganico.[42] The photos clearly depict Richthofen both with his *Pour le Mérite* (awarded 12 January 1917) and without his head wound (6 July), so they were taken during that timeframe. Richthofen's light flying gear suggests a warm weather month. Carganico was the commander of *FEA* 11, which was stationed outside of Breslau, from early 1917 through early 1918, so it is likely that the series originated there. Accordingly, the Halberstadt D.II in the background of MvR28 might have been the one that flipped over on Richthofen during his flight to Breslau on 31 May 1917. The man attending to something in the cockpit suggests that the plane had been flown recently. On the other hand, it merely could have been one of *FEA* 11's planes that just happened to be caught in the photographs.

Albatros D.III 789/17
(Mid-June 1917)
A brand new D.III 789/17 arrived for Richthofen at Roucourt on 2 May 1917 while he was away on leave. Richthofen returned to the front in mid-June and stated in his 18 June combat report that he had

used "Alb. D.III 789" to gain his 53rd victory. By 23 June, he had switched over to an Albatros D.V. Though it has long been speculated that 789/17 had a red-painted fuselage, we have no definite proof of this.

MvR30

MvR30: A lineup of *Jasta* 11 Albatros D.III and D.V aircraft on Roucourt airfield. The unit began to receive its D.Vs in late May 1917. The D.III third from right appears to have had a completely overpainted fuselage similar to "Le Petit Rouge." Unlike that plane, the manufacturer's logo on the rudder was covered over too, which could mean that it was 789/17 and not "Le Petit Rouge." This is pure speculation, however.

Albatros D.V 1177/17
(Late June through early July 1917)
The first examples of the new Albatros D.V model began to be delivered to *Jasta* 11 on 21 May 1917.[43]

Shortly after using 789/17 for his 53rd victory on 18 June, Richthofen began to fly D.V 1177/17, as noted in the combat reports for his 54th through 56th victories of 23–25 June.[44] Though two of those

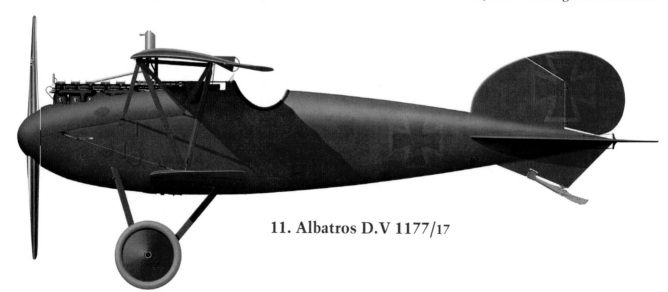

11. Albatros D.V 1177/17

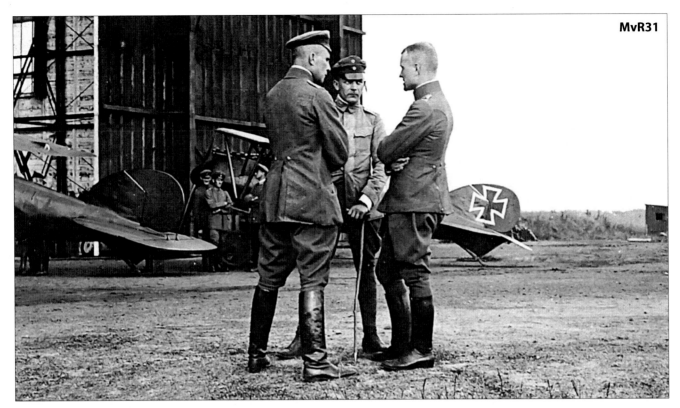

MvR31: This image has Richthofen (right) speaking with *Oblt.* Martin Gerlich (middle) of *Kampfgeschwader* 3 and his CO, *Hptm.* Rudolf Kleine (left). The large hangar in the background identifies the location as Gontrode, Belgium. Because *JG* 1 moved to the Belgian sector at Markebeke (near Kortrijk) on 2 July and Richthofen does not show any signs of his head wound of 6 July, the snapshot was taken sometime between those dates. Two *JG* 1 Albatros D.V aircraft are parked behind the men.

MvR32: This photo offers a more expansive view of the two *JG* 1 aircraft that were parked in front of *KG* 3 Gotha bombers that day. All the surfaces displayed by the fighter in the center have been overpainted – presumably red, because of Richthofen's presence in front of it. This and the fact that Richthofen had reported using a red D.V 1177/17 just before his fighter wing's move to Belgium points to this being that aircraft.

reports characterized the plane only as having a "red body," photographic evidence suggests that 1177/17 was more or less completely red (though the undersurfaces of the wings could have remained light blue). MvR31–32 capture Richthofen at Gontrode with a completely overpainted D.V in the background. MvR32 demonstrates that the images occurred after *JG* 1 had moved to Markebeke (2 July) but before Richthofen was wounded in the head (6 July). We know of no other predominantly red D.V that Richthofen flew at the time, so the one in these photos may have been 1177/17. The D.V

80

parked next to it sports an overpainted fuselage and wheel covers but the national insignia on its tail remained untouched. It looks very similar to D.V 2059/17, which Richthofen showed off to *Gen.* Erich Ludendorff when he visited *Jasta* 11 at Markebeke on 19 August 1917 (see MvR40–41 below); however, a detailed comparison demonstrates that they were not the same aircraft.

Albatros D.V ("hood, tail, decks red")
(2–6 July 1917)
Evidently, something happened to 1177/17 because Richthofen used another D.V on 2 July

for his 57th victory and again on 6 July when he was shot down and wounded. His combat report described it as "Alb. D.V, hood, tail, decks red." Richthofen's combat reports began to record his aircraft serial numbers in June 1917, yet this report uncharacteristically omitted it. MvR33–34 are previously unpublished pictures of this plane, taken during a visit to what might have been Moorsele airfield, where both *Flieger-Abteilung* 32 and *Marine-Flieger-Land-Abteilung* II were stationed in the summer of 1917.[45] MvR35–36 are two snapshots of the plane at the site of Richthofen's emergency landing just south of Wervicq-Sud.

MvR33

MvR33–34: Richthofen flew the plane he was later shot down in for a visit to another airfield (possibly Moorsele). The first image has Richthofen standing just behind the tail as the plane sits on the ground. The second shows Richthofen taking off.

MvR34

MvR33 Blowup

MvR35–36: Two pictures of Albatros D.V "hood, tail, decks red" after a grazing shot to the head had forced Richthofen to make an emergency landing in it within view of Wervicq-Sud. The second image clearly shows how the upper surfaces of its wings had been overpainted in red.

MvR34 Blowup

MvR35

MvR36

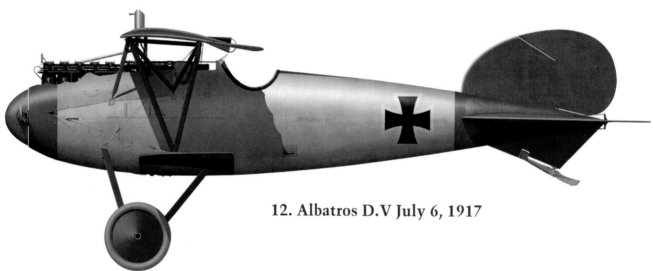

12. Albatros D.V July 6, 1917

Albatros D.V
(Sometime during 2–6 July 1917)
MvR37–38 tell us that Richthofen used a different Albatros D.V to visit Moorsele at some point between *JG* 1's move to Markebeke (2 July) and his being shot down and wounded (6 July).[46] It appears to have been the same plane later flown by *Lt.* Franz Müller after his arrival at *Jasta* 11 on 19 July 1917. Müller's plane was photographed as part of a *Jasta* 11 lineup. MvR39 shows that he had the tail from the horizontal stabilizer back repainted in white or another light color.

MvR37–38: Richthofen sits in the cockpit of an Albatros D.V during an early July 1917 visit to Moorsele airfield. The nose of the plane from the cockpit forward (see image in Ferko, *Richthofen*, p.34), the wheel covers and the rear of the fuselage and tail (but not the rudder) were probably painted red. Someone accompanied Richthofen in an Albatros D.III (OAW) that had a distinctive square patch underneath the cockpit that Jim Miller has pointed out was a rigging sheet placed there by the manufacturer. We otherwise know the D.III was produced by OAW because photo MvR38 shows that it sported a round rudder. (Second photo courtesy of Greg VanWyngarden)

MvR37

MvR38

MvR39: *Lt.* Franz Müller's Albatros D.V as it appeared in a lineup of *Jasta* 11 aircraft. He joined the unit on 19 July 1917 and remained with it until he was killed in a flying accident the following 27 October.

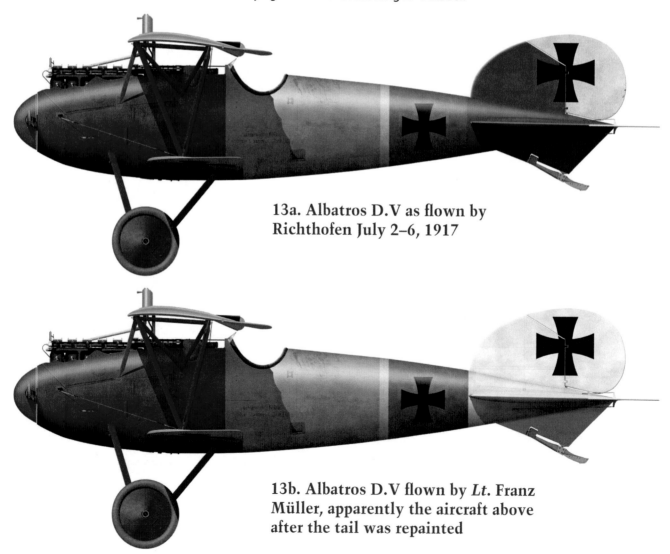

13a. Albatros D.V as flown by Richthofen July 2–6, 1917

13b. Albatros D.V flown by *Lt.* Franz Müller, apparently the aircraft above after the tail was repainted

Albatros D.V 2059/17?

(16 and 26 August 1917)

On 28 August 1917, Richthofen wrote his mother that he had made only two flights since returning to duty after his head wound of 6 July. He further stated that both had met with success, so he was referring to his 58th victory of 16 August and his 59th of 26 August. The combat report for his 58th has been lost and the one for his 59th (or at least its transcription) never specified the type or serial number of the plane he flew on that occasion. Circumstantial evidence points to it having been D.V 2059/17 because that

MvR40: Albatros D.V 2059/17 is put on prominant display during *Gen.* Erich Ludendorff's visit to Markebeke on 19 August 1917. In the center of the group of men to the left, Ludendorff is facing the camera and speaking to *Hptm.* Helmuth Wilberg, *Kofl* (Aviation Staff Officer) for the 4th Army to which *JG* 1 was attached, and Richthofen (bandaged head under service cap). At right is a lineup of *Jasta* 11 pilots (left to right): *Oblt.* Wilhelm Reinhard, unknown (but probably *Lt.* Wilhelm Bockelmann), *Lt.* Gisbert-Wilhelm Groos, *Lt.* Eberhardt Mohnicke, *Lt.* Karl-August von Schoenebeck, *Lt.* Carlos Meyer Baldó, *Lt.* Franz Müller, *Lt.* Eberhard Stapenhorst, *Lt.* Hans-Georg von der Osten. *Lt.* Krantz, Wilberg's adjutant, stands alone between the two groups.

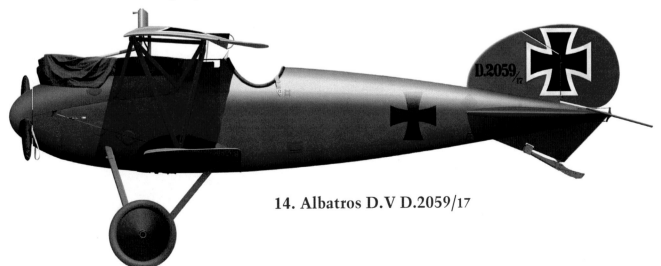

14. Albatros D.V D.2059/17

MvR41

MvR41: Ludendorff is now shaking hands with Meyer Baldó as Richthofen (standing between them) watches. Wilberg is in the center in front of three men wearing overcoats, while his adjutant, *Lt.* Krantz, stands off to the left.

fighter was paraded for *Gen.* Erich Ludendorff when he visited *Jasta* 11's airfield near Markebeke on 19 August 1917 – a date that falls between those two victories. MvR40–41 are two photographs taken during Ludendorff's visit.

MvR40 Blowup

Fokker F.I 102/17

(28 August—5 September 1917)

Fokker F.I 102/17 was delivered to Markebeke on 28 August 1917. MvR42–43 are two of a series of photographs taken when Richthofen showed the new plane off three days later to several dignitaries headed by German Chancellor Georg Michaelis. Richthofen's combat reports specifiy that he took it into combat the next day and achieved successes 60 and 61 in it on 1 and 3 September. Before Richthofen left the front on an enforced leave on 6 September, Anthony Fokker took movies of the plane that can still be viewed today.[47] *Oblt.* Kurt Wolff took over the triplane after Richthofen's departure and it was destroyed when Wolff was killed in it on 15 September 1917.

MvR42

MvR42: Richthofen stands off to the side as Anthony Fokker, sitting in F.I 102/17's cockpit, converses with *Generalmajor* Friedrich Karl von Lossberg (Chief of Staff of the 4th Army to which *JG* 1 was attached) at Markebeke on 31 August 1917. Next over from Richthofen to the right are *Oblt.* Karl Bodenschatz (*JG* 1 Adjutant) and *Lt.* Hans Adam (*Jasta* 6 CO).

MvR43

MvR43: F.I 102/17 and an Albatros D.V (2059/17 on display again?) rest in the background as Anthony Fokker (left) prepares to film some of the day's events. Speaking to Fokker is German Chancellor Georg Michaelis (white tabs on collar) while Richthofen stands at attention just right of Michaelis.

MvR43 Blowup

MvR44

MvR45

MvR44–47: Four views of F.I 102/17 at its hangar at Markebeke airfield. (First photo courtesy of Terry Phillips; second photo courtesy of Greg VanWyngarden)

MvR46

MvR48–49: Kurt Wolff had a forced landing in F.I 102/17 and these two pictures captured the aftermath. (Photos courtesy of Greg VanWyngarden and Terry Phillips)

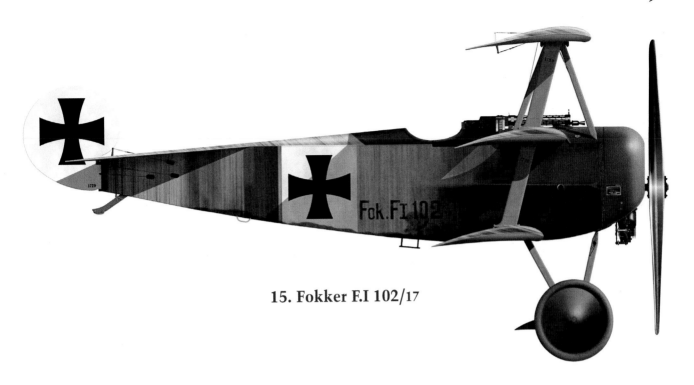

15. Fokker F.I 102/17

MvR49

Albatros C.IX

(6 September 1917 – ?)

"... Manfred telegraphed that he would be arriving by air in the afternoon. We waited on the small parade ground. The red plane, which is now his private property, appeared at 6:00. In the final glow of a clear September day, it gave the impression of having emerged from the middle of the sun. Manfred flew just once over the city, where he was noticed and greeted with great jubilation."[48]

Richthofen's mother wrote this passage after his visit in mid-October 1917.[49] Anthony Fokker filmed Richthofen's departure from Markebeke on 6 September in a dark-colored Albatros C.IX piloted by *Lt.* Eberhardt Mohnicke. Presumably, this was the "red plane" that Richthofen's mother watched as it arrived at Schweidnitz. Though we cannot be certain that he was at the controls at that time, we know that Richthofen flew the plane characterized as his "private property" on at least one other occasion. MvR50–54 show Richthofen during one of his stopovers at *FEA* 5's Hannover airfield and he can clearly be seen in the pilot's seat. MvR56 is a fun photo depicting brother Lothar showing

MvR50

16. Albatros C.IX

the plane off to the woman he would later marry in 1919, Countess Doris Katherina Margarete von Keyserlingk. There is little doubt that the Fokker films and these photos involved the same aircraft because only three Albatros C.IXs were ever built.

MvR51

MvR52

MvR50–54: In the first two photos, Richthofen clambers up into the cockpit of his Albatros C.IX using a cabane strut as a handhold. In the next two images, he sits at the controls while his companion settles into the back seat. The last view catches the plane as it takes off from Hannover airfield. (First photo courtesy of Thomas Genth)

MvR54

MvR55: Richthofen's Albatros C.IX undergoes an overhaul.

MvR56: Lothar von Richthofen and his future wife, Countess Doris Katherina Margarete von Keyserlingk, sit in brother Manfred's private plane. Evidently, Lothar treated her to a ride in it.

Fokker Dr.I 114/17
(23–30 October 1917)

"*Rittmstr.* and *Lt. Frhr.* v. Richthofen had emergency landings at 9:50 near Zilverberg, both uninjured. The *Rittmeister's* machine (Fokker Dr.I 114/17) totaled; the other machine undamaged."[50]

One week after Richthofen's return to the front on 23 October 1917, he suffered this accident while attempting to land beside brother Lothar's machine, which had set down due to engine failure. The reverse of MvR57 simply states "*Fockker* [sic] *Dreidecker Rittm. v. Richthofen*" ("Fockker triplane *Rittm.* v. Richthofen") and shows an obviously distressed Dr.I in standard late-1917 finish. It seems likely that it captured Dr.I 114/17 on the ground near Zilberberg following Richthofen's crash landing. Under magnification, a wire can be seen wrapped around both of the plane's starboard interplane struts – an indication that it had hit some wiring on the way in, causing the crash.

MvR57 Blowup

MvR57: A likely photo of Richthofen's Dr.I 114/17 on the ground after crashing near Zilverberg. It appears to have suffered that fate as a result of colliding with some wiring (see blowup) during what otherwise should have been a routine landing.

MvR57

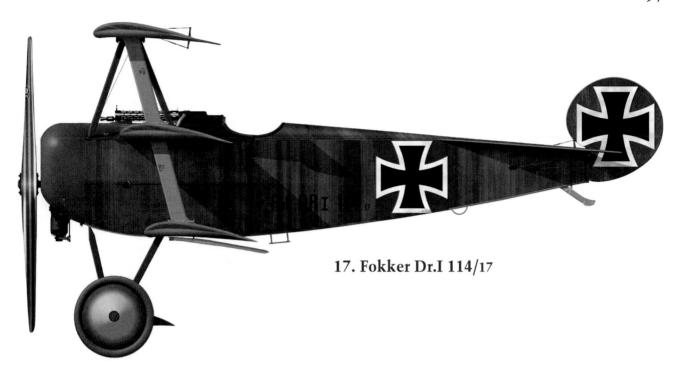

17. Fokker Dr.I 114/17

Albatros D.V 4693/17
(November—7 December 1917)
Coincidental with Richthofen's unfortunate incident in Dr.I 114/17, two pilots lost their lives on 30 and 31 October after their triplanes suffered upper wing failures. The type was subsequently grounded pending further investigation, which meant that Richthofen had to return to flying an Albatros D.V. His combat reports for 23 and 30 November (victories 62 and 63) respectively described that plane as "Alb. D.V.4693/17; red hood, red tail" and "Albatross [sic] D.V. 4693/17; red body, red tail."[51] At present, no photos of this airplane are known to exist.

Pfalz Dr.I 3050/17
(Sometime during 13–19 December 1917)
JG 1's war journal recorded that Richthofen was ordered to the Pfalz aircraft works at Speyer on 12 December and that he returned on 20 December 1917.[52] During that time, he had the opportunity to test fly the company's second triplane prototype, Dr.I 3050/17. The type had elicited much interest because during August 1917 flight testing, it had reached 5,000 meters in just 11.5 minutes whereas the Albatros D.V needed 35 minutes to do the same.[53] Nevertheless, it was plagued by low speed and engine reliability issues and never made its mark as a first-line fighter.

MvR58

MvR58–59: Two snapshots of Richthofen sitting in the cockpit of Dr.I 3050/17 when he tested it at Pfalz's aircraft works at Speyer sometime during 13–19 December 1917. In the image above, Richthofen is accompanied by Pfalz Company test pilot Ernst Schlegel (atop fuselage, far left). (Photos courtesy of Jack Herris)

MvR59

RI3050/17

MvR60: Richthofen had quite an audience during his test run. Standing in front of the Pfalz Dr.I (left to right): *Lt.* Hans Auer (former CO of *Jasta* 32, perhaps a member of *Kogenluft* or *Idflieg* staff), Ernst Everbusch (Pfalz Co. co-owner), *Hptm.* Willy Meyer (*Kogenluft*), *Hptm.* Albert Mühlig-Hofmann (*Idflieg*), *Lt.* Constantin Krefft (*JG* 1 Technical Officer), Richthofen, *Oblt.* Fritz von Falkenhayn (*Kogenluft*), *Hptm.* Adolf *Ritter* von Tutschek (former *Jasta* 12 CO, future *Geschwaderführer* of *JG* 2), *Dipl.-Ing.* Ernst Schlegel (Pfalz Co.), Alfred Everbusch (Pfalz Co. co-owner).

MvR60

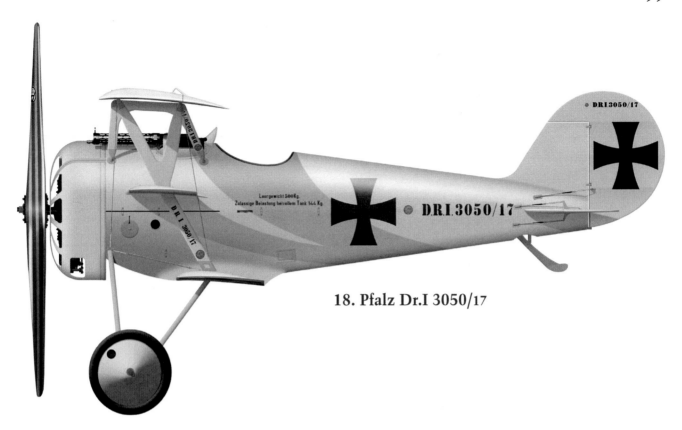

18. Pfalz Dr.I 3050/17

Fokker V.11
(23 and late January 1918)

Germany's first fighter trial competition began on 21 January 1918 at Adlershof field outside of Berlin and continued until 12 February 1918.[54] At Richthofen's suggestion, frontline fighter pilots were invited to participate in the trials, flying the prototypes and offering their opinions on their suitability for combat. Richthofen probably flew many of the types entered in the competition, but it is specifically known that he flew Fokker's V.11 prototype on 23 January 1918 and found it unstable. After Fokker's team worked through the weekend to make certain modifications (e.g., lengthening the fuselage) Richthofen flew it again before he went home at the end of the month.[55] Richthofen gave the new version his blessing and the type was eventually developed into the highly successful Fokker D.VII.

MvR61

MvR62

MvR61–62: Two pictures of Fokker's V.11 prototype before modifications were made to it to make it more stable. We do not know how it appeared when Richthofen flew it for the first time at the fighter trial competition. (Photos courtesy of Jack Herris)

MvR63–64: Two photographs of Fokker's V.11 prototype after its fuselage had been lengthened to increase its stability in flight. Movies that Fokker took at the fighter trial competition indicate that this is how the plane appeared when Richthofen flew it for the second time. (Photos courtesy of Jack Herris)

MvR63

MvR64

Fokker Dr.I 152/17
(12–18 March 1918)
According to his combat reports, Richthofen's next three victories (64–66) were achieved in Fokker Dr.I

152/17 with *"rotes oberes Tragdeck, rote Haube, rote Laufräder u. roter Schwanz"* ("red upper deck, red cowling, red wheels and red tail").[56] These successes occurred on 12, 13 and 18 March.

MvR65: This picture of Fokker Dr.I 152/17 clearly matches the description of it given in Richthofen's 64th–66th combat reports. (photo courtesy of Greg VanWyngarden)

MvR65

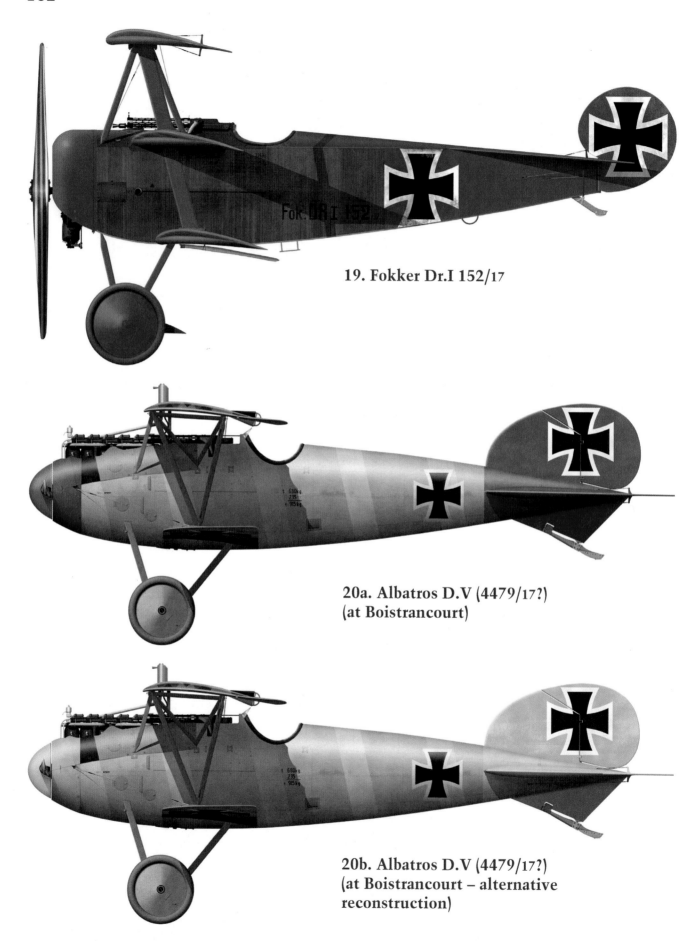

19. Fokker Dr.I 152/17

20a. Albatros D.V (4479/17?)
(at Boistrancourt)

20b. Albatros D.V (4479/17?)
(at Boistrancourt – alternative
reconstruction)

Albatros D.V
(13 March 1918)

The late A.E. Ferko stated that MvR66–67 were snapped during a 13 March 1918 visit to *Jasta* 5 at Boistrancourt.[57] That airfield was only a little more than 5 kilometers away from *JG* 1's base near Awoingt and Richthofen had gone there to attend the memorial service for *Jasta* 5's *Lt.* Wilhelm Gürke, who had been killed in action on 10 March (see photo on page 41 above). Death must have been on Richthofen's mind that day because earlier that morning, his brother Lothar had crashed while trying to reach Awoingt after his upper wing had collapsed during a dogfight at the front. Richthofen flew to the crash site to investigate for himself and was later reassured that Lothar's injuries, though serious, would not be fatal.[58]

The D.V that Richthofen flew to Boistrancourt seems to have been a *Jasta* 4 aircraft. As a unit marking, *Jasta* 4 had adopted a black ribbon that spiraled around the fuselage from nose to tail; and the plane in MvR66–67 shows evidence of that spiral having been repainted in an attempt to cover it up.

MvR66

MvR66: Richthofen salutes an officer as *Jasta* 5 CO *Oblt.* Richard Flashar (bespectacled man) observes from behind. The D.V Richthofen used to fly to Boistrancourt to attend the memorial service for *Jasta* 5's *Lt.* Wilhelm Gürke is in the background. (Photo courtesy of Jim Miller)

MvR67: Richthofen powers up the engine of the D.V he flew to Boistrancourt. Since its former *Jasta* 4 markings had been painted over, it appears that the plane had become either a *Jasta* 11 or *JG* 1 "hack" that was used for transport behind the lines. (Photo courtesy of Jim Miller)

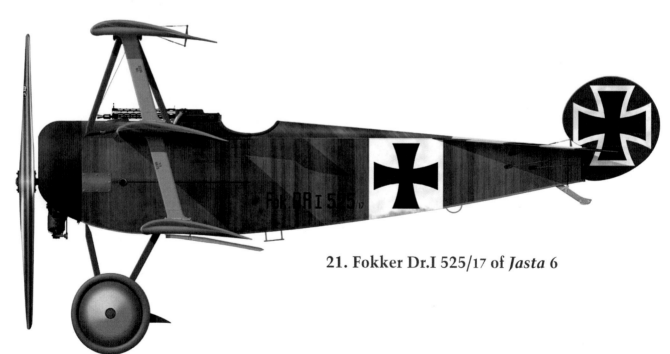

21. Fokker Dr.I 525/17 of *Jasta* 6

Fokker Dr.I
(17 March 1918)
Richthofen visited *Jasta* 5 on another occasion – 17 March 1918, according to A.E. Ferko.[59] MvR68–69

are two pictures taken of his mount that day: *Jasta* 6's 525/17 with a black cowl, black and white striped tailplane (above and below), and possibly black (or yellow or even red) upper wingtip surfaces.

MvR68

MvR68: A photograph of *Jasta* 6 triplane 525/17 Richthofen flew to *Jasta* 5 on 17 March 1918.

MvR69: Richthofen converses with members of *Jasta* 5 over the fuselage of the *Jasta* 6 Dr.I he used to visit them. Personnel left to right: Richthofen, a mechanic, *Lt.* Hans Joachim von Hippel, *Oblt.* Richard Flashar, unknown, *Lt.* Hans Schloemer, *Lt.* Wilhelm Lehmann. (Photo courtesy of Greg VanWyngarden)

MvR69

Fokker Dr.I 161/17
(21 March 1918)
During yet another visit to *Jasta* 5 – this time on 21

March 1918 – Richthofen flew Fokker Dr.I 161/17 to Boistrancourt.

MvR70

MvR70: Richthofen sits in the cockpit of Fokker Dr.I 161/17 at Boistrancourt airfield. Two more candid snapshots of the same occasion can be seen in Ferko, *Richthofen*, p.59. Judging from these images, this triplane probably bore the same markings as 127/17 and 477/17: red cowl, red tail and rudder, red wheels, red upper deck. (photo courtesy of Greg VanWyngarden)

MvR71

Fokker Dr.I 477/17
   (24 March–2 April 1918)
Richthofen primarily used Dr.I 477/17 over the course of his next 10 victories: numbers 67–70, 72–73, 75, and 77–78. Like most of his triplanes up to this time, it was described as having a "red upper deck, red hood, red wheels and red tail" in his combat reports.[60] Unfortunately, no known photo conclusively shows 477/17.[61]

Fokker Dr.I 127/17
   (27 March—2 April 1918)
For victories 71, 74, and 76, Richthofen flew Dr.I 127/17. MvR71 is an image of it before it had been painted to have the "red upper deck, red hood, red wheels and red tail" mentioned in his combat reports. MvR72–73 are two photos of it with that color scheme.

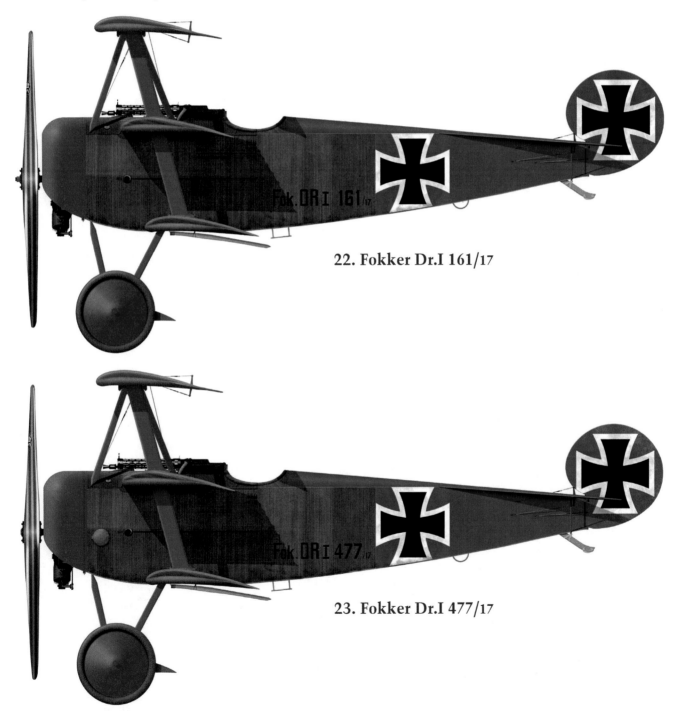

22. Fokker Dr.I 161/17

23. Fokker Dr.I 477/17

MvR71: A ground crew tends to Dr.I 127/17, which had not yet had its upper deck, hood, wheels, and tail painted red. (Photo courtesy of Jim Miller)

MvR72–73: Two snapshots of Dr.I 127/17 at the end of a lineup of triplanes at Léchelle airfield. By this time, it had been painted in Richthofen's red color scheme. In the first photo, Richthofen (marked with an "x") can be seen strolling toward the plane and a ground crewman who is holding his well-known fur boots. (Photos courtesy of Greg VanWyngarden)

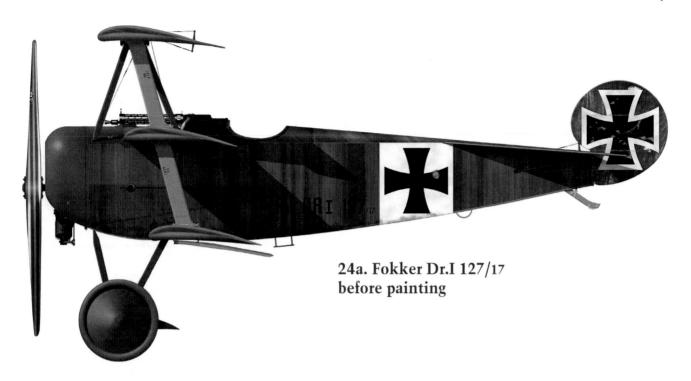

24a. Fokker Dr.I 127/17
before painting

24b. Fokker Dr.I 127/17
after painting

Fokker Dr.I 425/17
(20–21 April 1918)

After *JG* 1's move to Cappy airfield on 12 April 1918, Richthofen switched over to flying Dr.I 425/17, which was described in the combat reports for his final two victories on 20 April as "*roter Anstrich*" ("red paint").[62] This is the aircraft in which Richthofen was killed on 21 April. Various photographs show us that it initially had an all-red color scheme but then later had a white rudder with the new *Balkenkreuz* insignia applied to it.[63]

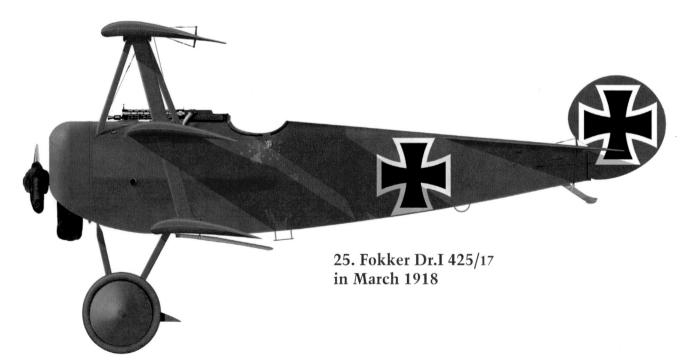

25. Fokker Dr.I 425/17
in March 1918

MvR74–75: These two views of Dr.I 425/17 before its Iron Cross insignia were replaced with *Balkenkreuz* insignia demonstrate that it originally was red all over except for the white outlines on its insignia. Note the scarring shaped like an inverted "V" just underneath the cockpit coaming in the first image.

MvR76: Dr.I 425/17, now displaying *Balkenkreuz* insignia and a white rudder, rests under guard. The same inverted "V" scarring as noted above can be seen just over the shoulder of the man standing at center.

MvR76

**26. Fokker Dr.I 425/17
in April 1918**

Fokker Dr.I 152/17?
   (April 1918?)
As the caption for MvR78 says, this Dr.I is supposed to have been one of Richthofen's machines and was displayed as such in Berlin's Zeughaus Museum between the wars. Many believe it was 152/17 after it had been painted completely red – and their arguments are good – but there really is no way to absolutely verify this. Evidently, the plane was either in the process of a *Balkenkreuz* conversion or some of the insignia's white background had simply flaked off before it was sent back to Germany for display.

MvR77: One of Richthofen's machines that many think was 152/17.

MvR78: The same plane, displaying the same markings, on display at Berlin's Zeughaus Museum after the war.

Endnotes

[1] For example, see James F. Miller, *Manfred von Richthofen: The Aircraft, Myths and Accomplishments of 'The Red Baron'*, Greg VanWyngarden, *Von Richthofen's Flying Circus*, and Greg VanWyngarden, *'Richthofen's Circus': Jagdgeschwader Nr 1*.

[2] *Mein Kriegstagebuch*, pp.56–57; *Mother of Eagles*, pp.82–83.

[3] *Der rote Kampfflieger* (1933), p.64; *The Red Baron*, p.26.

[4] See p.10 above.

[5] *Richthofen*, p.5. Presumably, it was because of the black cat insignia on the side of the plane. Peter Supf (*Das Buch der deutschen Fluggeschichte* Vol.2, p.437) related that Zeumer was known among his comrades as the *"schwarze Katz"* ("black cat").

[6] *Der rote Kampfflieger* (1933), pp.82–83; *The Red Baron*, p.39.

[7] My thanks to Jack Herris for this possible identification.

[8] E.g., see Ferko, *Richthofen*, pp.8 and 9.

[9] Ibid., p.9.

[10] See above, p.14.

[11] For two other photos of the wreck, see Ferko, *Richthofen*, p.10.

[12] *Der rote Kampfflieger* (1917), pp.76–78; *The Red Baron*, pp.43–45.

[13] *Mein Kriegstagebuch*, p.82; *Mother of Eagles*, p.100.

[14] The D.Is at far right and left had overpainted fuselages as well, and the one at far right similarly left the panel behind the spinner and a patch for its serial number (427/16) untouched.

[15] Franks, Giblin, & McCrery, *Under the Guns of the Red Baron*, p.23. It was not uncommon for RFC pilots to mistakenly refer to German fighters as Nieuport-types.

[16] See Ferko, *Richthofen*, p.13. As far as we know, Richthofen's original combat reports no longer exist and we have only English translations from various sources to rely upon. The English version of Richthofen's 27 December 1916 combat report, obtained by the Royal Air Force from author Floyd Gibbons in 1927 and later supplied to London's National Archives, gives serial number "D.481." Heinz Nowarra in his and Kimbrough Brown's book, *von Richthofen and the Flying Circus* (Fallbrook: Aero Publishers, 1964) (p.37) listed it as 491/16 but the source of that information is unknown.

[17] Transcript in London's National Archives.

[18] Ferko, *Richthofen*, p.79.

[19] It has sometimes been offered that *"Le Petit Rouge"* bore serial number 789/17. This is impossible, however, because that plane was ordered in March 1917 and delivered to *Jasta* 11 on 2 May. See Grosz, *Albatros D.III*, p.55 and Ferko, *Richthofen*, p.79.

[20] Transcript in London's National Archives.

[21] Franks, Giblin, & McCrery, *Under the Guns of the Red Baron*, p.63.

[22] Ibid., p.68. The authors did not quote their source directly, so the phrases quoted here actually come from their summary.

[23] Ibid., p.71. Same proviso as above.

[24] *Der rote Kampfflieger* (1917), pp.116, 114 and 115. The chapter heading lists the date only as "mid-March." Richthofen's statement at the end that he had achieved his 25th victory the same day has led some to conclude that he was shot down on 9 March. We know from other sources that Lübbert was wounded on 6 March, however, so this almost certainly is the correct date.

[25] Ferko, *Richthofen*, p.19. It appears that Lübbert made this entry after Richthofen had been promoted to *Oberleutnant* on 23 March 1917, which is understandable because Lübbert had been wounded on 6 March and probably did not get around to recording the day's events until later. Nevertheless, his entry was not very far removed because Lübbert met his death in air combat on 30 March 1917.

[26] Franks, Giblin & McCrery, *Under the Guns of the Red Baron*, p.72. Same proviso as in endnote 22.

[27] Ferko, *Richthofen*, p.15.

[28] Ibid., p.79.

[29] Ibid., p.20. Ferko did not name the source for this information, but given the context in which it was presented, it appears that it came from Lübbert's diary.

[30] Transcript in London's National Archives.

[31] My thanks to Jim Miller for pointing this out.

[32] Ferko, *Richthofen*, p.79.

[33] *Ein Heldenleben*, pp.221–22.

[34] In several of the many copies of MvR19 that exist, there are faint signs of a colored band behind the cockpit; however, unlike D.III 2006/16's appearance in MvR14–15, the rudder is dark. A paint can is visible on the ground near the tail of the plane, which suggests that it was in the process of being repainted – which could account for the dark rudder and less distinct fuselage band.

[35] Ferko, *Richthofen*, p.21.

[36] Photos of Schaefer's D.III will be featured in an upcoming volume of this series.

[37] *Jasta* 11's Hans-Georg von der Osten summed it up this way: "Sometimes it even happened that your own plane was kaputt and you took another plane with another insignia on it. You told the others 'Today my bird has such and such markings' and you took off..." (*Cross and Cockade* 15:3, p.221)

[38] *Der rote Kampfflieger* (1917), pp.159–60; *The Red Baron*, p.94.

[39] *Cross & Cockade* 15:3, p.219.

[40] *Mein Kriegstagebuch*, pp.113–14; *Mother of Eagles*, pp.127–28.

[41] *Ein Heldenleben*, pp.223–24.

[42] See Ferko, *Richthofen*, p.36 and *Cross & Cockade* 10:2, p.106 for additional photos.

[43] Ferko, *Richthofen*, p.79.

[44] The combat report for his 55th victory is dated 26 June 1917 in the London National Archive's transcript and by its source, Floyd Gibbons, in *The Red Knight of Germany*, p.282. *Nachrichtenblatt* No.18 (*Over The Front* 19:1, p.89) gave the date as 24 June and a suitable candidate has been found on that date. Therefore, "26" June was either a typographical error or perhaps the date on which the success was subsequently confirmed.

[45] Another photograph taken during this visit can be seen in Ferko, *Richthofen*, p.38.

[46] Another picture taken during this visit can be seen in Ferko, *Richthofen*, p.36. Ferko was under the impression that Richthofen had piloted the Albatros D.III(OAW) seen behind him in that photo; however, note the light patch just to the right of Richthofen's arm. The same patch is visible in MvR37 on the D.III(OAW) that accompanied Richthofen's D.V. They are one and the same plane, piloted by someone else. In fact, that pilot can be seen entering (or exiting) the cockpit in Ferko's image.

[47] See endnote 66 for the prior section.

[48] *Mein Kriegstagebuch*, p.127; *Mother of Eagles*, p.138.

[49] See endnote 71 for the prior section.

[50] Bodenschatz, *Jagd in Flanderns Himmel*, p.162; *Hunting with Richthofen*, p.156.

[51] Transcript in London's National Archives.

[52] Bodenschatz, *Jagd in Flanderns Himmel*, p.166; *Hunting with Richthofen*, pp.162–63.

[53] For a detailed account and multiple photos of the Pfalz Dr.I, see Jack Herris, *Pfalz Aircraft of World War I*, pp.66–72, 136–37.

[54] For more information on this trial and the two that followed it, see Jack Herris, *Germany's Fighter Competitions of 1918*.

[55] See A.R. Weyl, *Fokker: The Creative Years*, pp.264–65.

[56] Bodenschatz, *Jagd in Flanderns Himmel*, p.171.

[57] *Richthofen*, p.58. Ferko did not reveal the source for this information.

[58] As reported by *Lt.* Friedrich Wilhelm Lübbert (brother of Hans-Georg Eduard Lübbert) in *Ein Heldenleben*, pp.313–14.

[59] *Richthofen*, p.59.

[60] Transcripts in London's National Archives.

[61] The question of whether or not one particular photo captured 477/17 (e.g, see Ferko, *Richthofen*, p.65 and Imrie, *The Fokker Triplane*, p.65) has been debated but not definitively resolved.

[62] Bodenschatz, *Jagd in Flanderns Himmel*, p.179.

[63] Photographs taken of Richthofen's wrecked 425/17 on 22 April indicate that the rudder had not been overpainted. It could have been recovered or replaced.

Right: This Steve Anderson watercolor depicts Manfred von Richthofen's 65th victory on 13 March 1918. Richthofen was flying Fokker Dr.I 152/17 when he shot down RFC No.73 Squadron's Sopwith Camel B2523, flown by Lt. Elmer E. Heath. Heath was wounded and taken prisoner.

Manfred von Richthofen – Military Service

Significant Dates

2 May 1892	Born in Breslau (now Wrocław, Poland)
Aug 1903	Enters Cadet Academy at Wahlstatt (now Legnickie Pole, Poland)
1909	Enters Senior Cadet Academy at Gross-Lichterfelde
1911	*Fahnenjunker* with *Ulanen-Regiment Kaiser Alexander III. von Russland (Westpreussisches) Nr.1*
1911	Attends War School in Berlin
19 Nov 1912	Commissioned *Leutnant*
End of May 1915	Assigned to *Flieger-Ersatz-Abteilung 7* for evaluation as observer
10 Jun 1915	Assigned to *Flieger-Ersatz-Abteilung 6* for observer training
21 Jun 1915	Assigned to *Feldflieger-Abteilung 69*
Late Aug 1915	Assigned to *Brieftauben-Abteilung Ostende*
10 Oct 1915	Makes solo flight
15 Nov 1915	Assigned to *Flieger-Ersatz-Abteilung 2* at Döberitz for pilot training
25 Dec 1915	Passes Pilot's Exam 3
16 Mar 1916	Assigned to *Kampstaffel 8 (Kagohl 2)*
15 Aug 1916	Invited by Oswald Boelcke to join *Jasta 2*
1 Sep 1916	Arrives at *Jasta 2*
17 Sep 1916	First victory
12 Jan 1917	Awarded *Pour le Mérite*
15 Jan 1917	CO of *Jasta 11*
23 Mar 1917	Promoted to *Oberleutnant*
7 Apr 1917	Promoted to *Rittmeister*
13 Apr 1917	Germany's Ace of Aces with 41st victory
24 Jun 1917	Commander of *Jagdgeschwader (JG) Nr.1*
7 Jul 1917	Wounded in action
25 Jul 1917	Resumed command of *JG 1*
20 Apr 1918	Final victory (#80)
21 Apr 1918	Killed in action
22 Apr 1918	Buried at Bertangles, France
2 May 1918	Memorial service in Berlin
1921	Reinterred at Fricourt, France
20 Nov 1925	Reinterred at Invalidenfriedhof, Berlin
1975	Reinterred at Südfriedhof, Wiesbaden

Service Units

1911–26 May 1915	*Ulanen-Regiment Kaiser Alexander III. von Russland (Westpreussisches) Nr.1*
27 May–9 Jun 1915	*Flieger-Ersatz-Abteilung 7*
10–20 Jun 1915	*Flieger-Ersatz-Abteilung 6*
21 Jun–late Aug 1915	*Feldflieger-Abteilung 69*
late Aug–late 1915	*Brieftauben-Abteilung Ostende*
late 1915	*Flieger-Ersatz-Abteilung 2*
Jan–15 Mar 1916	Unknown Berlin assignment
16 Mar–31 Aug 1916	*Kampstaffel 8 (Kagohl 2)*
1 Sep 1916–14 Jan 1917	*Jagdstaffel 2*
15 Jan–23 Jun 1917	*Jagdstaffel 11*
24 Jun 1917–21 Apr 1918	*Jagdgeschwader (JG) Nr.1*

Right: An *Ulanen-Regiment Kaiser Alexander III. von Russland (Westpreussisches) Nr.1* field-gray tunic of the type worn by Richthofen.

Awards

23 Sep 1914	Iron Cross, 2nd Class – Prussia
1915	Iron Cross, 1st Class – Prussia
21 Jun 1915*	Observer's Badge – Germany
25 Dec 1915**	Pilot's Badge – Germany
17 Sep 1916***	*Ehrenbecher* – Germany
9 Nov 1916****	Oval Silver Duke Carl Eduard Medal with Date Clasp and Swords – Saxe-Coburg-Gotha
11 Nov 1916	Royal Hohenzollern House Order, Knight's Cross with Swords – Prussia
12 Jan 1917	*Pour le Mérite* – Prussia
13 Apr 1917	Military Merit Order, Knight – Württemberg
16 Apr 1917	Military St. Henry Order, Knight's Cross – Saxony
29 Apr 1917	Military Merit Order, 4th Class with Swords – Bavaria*****
9 May 1917	Saxe-Ernestine House Order, Knight 1st Class with Swords – Saxon Duchies
13 Jan–9 May 1917ˣ	Military Merit Cross, 3rd Class with War Decoration – Austria-Hungary
13 Jan–early Jun 1917ˣˣ	Field Pilot's Badge, Army – Austria-Hungary
Mid-Jun 1917	Bravery Order, 4th Class (1st Degree) – Bulgaria
8 Aug 1917	Order of the Iron Crown, 3rd Class with War Decoration – Austria-Hungary
22 Sep 1917	Hanseatic Cross – Lübeck
24 Sep 1917	War Merit Cross, 2nd Class – Brunswick
25 Sep 1917	Hanseatic Cross – Hamburg
10 Oct 1917	Cross for Faithful Service, 2nd Class – Schaumburg-Lippe
13 Oct 1917	War Honor Cross for Heroic Act – Lippe
4 Nov 1917	War Medal – Ottoman Empire
27 Mar–11 Apr 1918	War Merit Cross, 2nd Class – Brunswickˣˣˣ
6 Apr 1918	Red Eagle Order, 3rd Class with Crown and Swords – Prussia
Unknown	General Honor Decoration "For Bravery" – Hesse
Unknownˣˣˣˣ	Hanseatic Cross – Bremen
Unknown	Liakat Medal in Silver – Ottoman Empire
Unknown	Imtiaz Medal in Silver – Ottoman Empire

Notes:

*This is an assumption based on his date of assignment to *Feldflieger-Abteilung* 69 as an observer

**This is an assumption based on the date of his passing the third and final Pilot's Exam

***This is an assumption based on the date of his first victory

****Awarded on 9 November; date clasp incorrectly marked "11.11."

*****Ordenskissen* displayed order with Crown and Swords; but Bavarian order records do not support such an award

ˣNot wearing decoration in PLM photo; listed among his awards in document dated 9 May 1917

ˣˣNot wearing decoration in PLM photo; wearing it in photo taken during early June 1917 visit to Austria-Hungary

ˣˣˣAwarded personally (and perhaps mistakenly) for second time by Duke Ernst August at Léchelle

ˣˣˣˣProbably close to other Hanseatic Cross awards in late September 1917

Right: Another portrait, probably post-war, of Richthofen painted by a now unknown artist. It was patterned after a photo that appeared on Sanke Card No.532. It is in a private collection.

Manfred von Richthofen Victory List

No.	Date	Aircraft	Location, Unit & Crew*
1	17 Sep 1916	FE.2b 7018	Villers-Plouich – RFC 11: 2Lt. LBF Morris (POW/DOW), Lt. T Rees (KIA)
2	23 Sep	Martinsyde G.100 7481	Beugny – RFC 27: Sgt. Herbert Bellerby (KIA)
3	30 Sep	FE.2b 6973	Frémicourt – RFC 11: Lt. Ernest C Lansdale (POW/DOW), Sgt. Albert Clarkson (KIA)
4	7 Oct	BE.12 6618	Equancourt – RFC 21: 2Lt. William C Fenwick (KIA)
5	16 Oct	BE.12 6580	Near Ytres – RFC 19: 2Lt. John Thompson (KIA)
6	25 Oct	BE.12 6629	Near Bapaume – RFC 21: 2Lt. Arthur J Fisher (KIA)
7	3 Nov	FE.2b 7010	Northeast of Grevillers Wood – RFC 18: Sgt. Cuthbert G Baldwin, 2Lt. George A Bentham (b-KIA)
8	9 Nov	BE.2c 2506	Beugny – RFC 12: 2Lt. Ian G Cameron (POW/DOI)
9	20 Nov	BE.2c 2767?	South of Grandcourt – RFC 15: 2Lt. James C Lees (WIA/POW), Lt. Thomas H Clarke (POW)?
10	20 Nov	FE.2b 4848	Near Gueudecourt – RFC 18: 2Lt. Gilbert S Hall (POW/DOW), 2Lt. George Doughty (KIA)
11	23 Nov	DH.2 5964	South of Bapaume – RFC 24: Maj. Lanoe G Hawker (KIA)
12	11 Dec	DH.2 5986	Mercatel – RFC 32: Lt. Benedict PG Hunt (WIA/POW)
13	20 Dec	DH.2 7927	Near Monchy[-au-Bois] – RFC 29: Capt. Arthur G Knight (KIA)
14	20 Dec	FE.2b A5446	Near Noreuil – RFC 18: 2Lt. Lionel G D'Arcy, SLt. Reginald C Whiteside (b-KIA)
15	27 Dec	FE.2b	Near Ficheux – ?
16	4 Jan 1917	Sopwith Pup	Near Metz-en-Couture – RNAS 8: FSLt. Allan S Todd (KIA)
17	23 Jan	FE.8 6388.4	Southwest of Lens – RFC 40: 2Lt. John Hay (KIA)
18	24 Jan	FE.2b 6997	Near Vimy – RFC 25: Capt. Oscar Greig (POW), Lt. John E MacLennan (b-POW)
19	1 Feb	BE.2d 6742	Southwest of Thélus – RFC 16: Lt. Percival W Murray (POW/DOW), Lt. Duncan J McRae (DOW)
20	14 Feb	BE.2d 6231	Near Lens-Hulloch Road – RFC 2: Lt. Cyril D Bennett (WIA/POW), 2Lt. Herbert A Croft (KIA)
21	14 Feb	BE.2c 2543	Near Mazingarbe – RFC 2: Capt. George C Bailey (WIA), 2Lt. George WB Hampton (OK)
22	4 Mar	BE.2d 5785?	North of Loos – RFC 2: Lt. James BE Crosbee (OK), Sgt. John E Prance (WIA)?
23	4 Mar	Sopwith Strutter A1108	Near Acheville – RFC 43: 2Lt. Herbert J Green, 2Lt. Alexander W Reid (b-KIA)
24	6 Mar	BE.2e A2785	Near Souchez – RFC 16: 2Lt. Gerald M Gosset-Bibby, Lt. Geoffrey JO Brichta (b-KIA)
25	9 Mar	DH.2 A2571	Between Roclincourt and Bailleul[-Sir-Bertholt] – RFC 29: 2Lt. Arthur J Pearson (KIA)
26	11 Mar	BE.2d 6232	Near La Folie Wood – RFC 2: 2Lt. James Smyth, 2Lt. Edward Byrne (b-KIA)
27	17 Mar	FE.2b A5439	Near Oppy – RFC 25: Lt. Arthur E Boultbee, 2AM Frederick King (b-KIA)
28	17 Mar	BE.2e A2814	West of Vimy – RFC 16: 2Lt. George M Watt, Sgt. Ernest A Howlett (b-KIA)
29	21 Mar	BE.2f A3154	North of Neuville[-Saint-Vaast] – RFC 16: FSgt. Sidney H Quicke, 2Lt. William J Lidsey (b-KIA)
30	24 Mar	SPAD 7 A6706	Near Givenchy[-en-Gohelle] – RFC 19: Lt. Richard P Baker (WIA/POW)
31	25 Mar	Nieuport 17 A6689	Near Tilloy-lès-Mofflaines – RFC 29: 2Lt. Christopher G Gilbert (POW)
32	2 Apr	BE.2d 5841	Farbus – RFC 13: Lt. Patrick JG Powell, 1AM Percy Bonner (b-KIA)
33	2 Apr	Sopwith Strutter A2401	East of Givenchy[-en-Gohelle] – RFC 43: 2Lt. Algernon P Warren (POW), Sgt. Reuel Dunn (KIA)
34	3 Apr	FE.2d A6382	Near Liévin – RFC 25: 2Lt. Donald P McDonald (POW), 2Lt. John IM O'Beirne (KIA)

No.	Date	Aircraft	Location, Unit & Crew*
35	5 Apr	Bristol F.2a A3340	Near Lewarde – RFC 48: 2Lt. Arthur N Lechler (WIA/POW), 2Lt. Herbert DK George (WIA/POW/DOW)
36	5 Apr	Bristol F.2a A3343	Near Cuincy – RAF 48: Lt. Alfred T Adams (POW), Lt. Donald J Stewart (WIA/POW)
37	7 Apr	Nieuport 17 A6645	Near Mercatel – RFC 60: 2Lt. George O Smart (KIA)
38	8 Apr	Sopwith Strutter A2406	Near Farbus – RFC 43: 2Lt John S Heagerty (POW), Lt. Leonard H Cantle (KIA)
39	8 Apr	BE.2g A2815	Near Vimy – RFC 16: 2Lt. Keith I MacKenzie, 2Lt. Guy Everingham (b-KIA)
40	11 Apr	BE.2c 2501	Near Willerval – RFC 13: Lt. Edward CE Derwin, Gunner H Pierson (b-WIA)
41	13 Apr	RE.8 A3190	Between Vitry and Brebières – RFC 59: Capt. James M Stuart, Lt. Maurice H Wood (b-KIA)
42	13 Apr	FE.2b A831	Between Monchy-le-Preux and Feuchy – RFC 11: Sgt. James A Cunniffe, 2AM WJ Batten (b-WIA)
43	13 Apr	FE.2b 4997	Near Noyelles-Godault – RFC 25: 2Lt. Allan H Bates, Sgt. William A Barnes (b-KIA)
44	14 Apr	Nieuport 17 A6796	South of Bois-Bernard – RFC 60: Lt. William O Russell (POW)
45	16 Apr	BE.2e A3156	Between Bailleul[-Sir-Bertholt] and Gavrelle – RFC 13: 2Lt. Alphonso Pascoe (WIA), 2Lt. Frederick S Andrews (DOW)
46	22 Apr	FE.2b A820 OR 7020	Near Lagnicourt – RFC 11: Lt. CA Parker (OK), 2Lt. JEB Hesketh (DOW); OR RFC 11: Lt. William F Fletcher, Lt. Waldemar Franklin (b-WIA)
47	23 Apr	BE.2f A3168	Near Méricourt – RFC 16: 2Lt. Eric A Welch, Sgt. Amos G Tollervey (b-KIA)
48	28 Apr	BE.2e 7221	East of Pelves – RFC 13: Lt. Reginald W Follit (DOW), 2Lt. Frederick J Kirkham (WIA/POW)
49	29 Apr	SPAD 7 B1573	Near Lecluse – RFC 19: Lt. Richard Applin (KIA)
50	29 Apr	FE.2b 4898	Near Pariville – RFC 18: Sgt. George Stead, Cpl. Alfred Beebee (b-KIA)
51	29 Apr	BE.2e A2738	Near Rœux – RFC 12: Lt. David E Davies, Lt. George H Rathbone (b-KIA)
52	29 Apr	Sopwith Triplane N5463	Between Billy-Montigny and Sallaumines – RNAS 8: FSLt. Albert E Cuzner (KIA)
53	18 Jun	RE.8 A4617	North of Ypres (Ieper) – RFC 53: Lt ME Newton, 2Lt. HM Jackson (b-KIA)
54	23 Jun	SPAD 7 B1530	North of Ypres (Ieper) – RFC 23: 2Lt. Robert W Farquhar (OK)
55	24 Jun	DH.4 A7473	South of Becelaere – RFC 57: Capt. Norman G McNaughton, Lt. Angus H Mearns (b-KIA)
56	25 Jun	RE.8 A3847	Near Le Bizet – RFC 53: Lt. Leslie S Bowman, 2Lt. James E Power-Clutterbuck (b-KIA)
57	2 Jul	RE.8 A3538	Deûlémont – RFC 53: Sgt. Hubert A Whatley, 2Lt. Frank GB Pascoe (b-KIA)
58	16 Aug	Nieuport 23 A6611	Southwest of Houthhulst Forest – RFC 29: 2Lt. William HT Williams (WIA/POW/DOW)
59	26 Aug	SPAD 7 B3492	Between Poelkapelle and Langemark – RFC 19: 2Lt. Coningsby P Williams (KIA)
60	1 Sep	RE.8 B782	Near Zonnebeke – RFC 6: Lt. John BC Madge (WIA/POW), 2Lt. Walter Kember (KIA)
61	3 Sep	Sopwith Pup B1795.Z	South of Bousbecque – RFC 46: Lt. Algernon F Bird (POW)
62	23 Nov	DH.5 A9299	Bourlon Wood – RFC 64: Lt. James AV Boddy (WIA)
63	30 Nov	SE.5a B644	Near Mœuvres – RFC 41: Lt. Donald ADI MacGregor (KIA)
64	12 Mar 1918	Bristol F.2b B1251	Near Le Catelet – RFC 62: 2Lt. Leonard CF Clutterbuck (WIA/POW), 2Lt. Henry J Sparks (POW)
65	13 Mar	Sopwith Camel B2523	Between Gonnelieu and Banteux – RFC 73: Lt. Elmer E Heath (WIA/POW)

No.	Date	Aircraft	Location, Unit & Crew*
66	18 Mar	Sopwith Camel B5243	Near Molain – RFC 54: 2Lt. William G Ivamy (POW)
67	24 Mar	SE.5a C1054?	Near Combles – RFC 41: Lt. John P McCone (KIA)?
68	25 Mar	Sopwith Camel C1562	Between Contalmaison and Albert – RFC 3: 2Lt. Donald Cameron (KIA)
69	26 Mar	SE.5a B511?	Wood south of Contalmaison – RFC 1: 2Lt. Allan M Denovan (KIA)?
70	26 Mar	RE.8 B742	Northeast of Albert – RFC 15: 2Lt. Vernon J Reading, 2Lt. Matthew Leggat (b-KIA)
71	27 Mar	Sopwith Camel C6733	North of Aveluy – RFC 73: Capt. Thomas S Sharpe (WIA/POW)
72	27 Mar	AWFK.8 B288?	West of Foucaucourt[-en-Santerre] – RFC 2: Lt. Edward T Smart, Lt. Kenneth P Barford (b-KIA)?
73	27 Mar	Sopwith Dolphin C4016?	North of Chuignolles – RFC 79: 2Lt. George H Harding (KIA)?
74	28 Mar	AWFK.8 C8444	Near Méricourt – RFC 82: 2Lt. Joseph B Taylor, 2Lt. Eric Betley (b-KIA)
75	2 Apr	RE.8 A3868	Northeast of Moreuil – RAF 52: 2Lt. Ernest D Jones, 2Lt. Robert F Newton (b-KIA)
76	6 Apr	Sopwith Camel D6491	Wood northeast of Villers-Bretonneux – RAF 46: Capt. Sydney P Smith (KIA)
77	7 Apr	Sopwith Camel D6550?	Near Hangard – RAF 73: 2Lt. Albert V Gallie (OK)?
78	7 Apr	Sopwith Camel D6554?	North of Villers-Bretonneux – RAF 73: Lt. Ronad GH Adams (WIA/POW)?
79	20 Apr	Sopwith Camel D6439	Bois de Hamel – RAF 3: Maj. Richard Raymond-Barker (KIA)
80	20 Apr	Sopwith Camel B7393	Northeast of Villers-Bretonneux – RAF 3: 2Lt. David G Lewis (POW)

*pilot listed first
b-   both occupants
DOI   died of injuries
DOW   died of wounds
KIA   killed in action
POW   prisoner of war
WIA   wounded in action

Left: A fuselage insignia removed from Fokker Dr.I 425/17 and currently on display in Australia.

Above: An example of an epaulette bearing the insignia of *Ulanen-Regiment Kaiser Alexander III. von Russland (Westpreussisches) Nr.1.* Richthofen often attached similar insignia to his *Ulanka* (Uhan tunic) shoulder boards.

Above & Below: A coin issued by Ludwig Christian Lauer in 1917 to honor Richthofen.

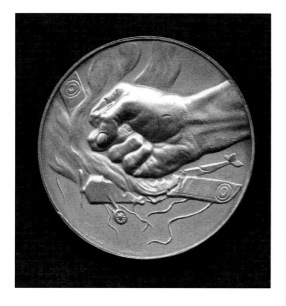

Right: An *Ulanen-Regiment Kaiser Alexander III. von Russland (Westpreussisches) Nr.*1 dress tunic of the type worn by Richthofen. (The helmet, though an authentic *Tschapka* of the period, is not from that regiment.) This is what Richthofen wore for the photos seen on pages 4 and 6.

Color Profile Commentaries
By Greg VanWyngarden

1. AEG G.II G.6/15, flown by *Lt.* Georg Zeumer with *Lt.* Manfred von Richthofen as observer, *B.A.O.* According to the late historian A.E. Ferko, this AEG was on the strength of *B.A.O.* (*Brieftauben-Abteilung Ostende*) at Ghistelles in Flanders during Richthofen's time there as an observer for his friend Zeumer. The arched black cat seen painted on the fuselage was – according to Ferko – a reference to Zeumer's nickname of "the black cat" (as recorded by Peter Supf). Whatever the case, the cat emblem was a very early example of a personal marking on a German aircraft. If this was indeed the *Grosskampfflugzeug* in which Richthofen suffered the injury to his finger, then the photo (MvR1) must post-date that incident. Protective screens are visible in the photo adjacent to the forward cockpit, perhaps retro-fitted to prevent a recurrence of such an accident. Little is recorded about the finish of the early AEG G-types; however, we have chosen to portray this example as finished in natural-doped, unbleached gray-beige linen, with the plywood-covered nose and metal areas painted a matching color.

2. LFG Roland C.II flown by *Lt.* Manfred von Richthofen, *Kasta* 8 of *Kagohl* 2. Considerable uncertainty exists in regard to which Roland C.II *Walfisch* seen in the line-up photo (MvR2) of *Kasta* 8 was flown by Richthofen, and has been the topic for much debate between contributors to this volume. A.E. Ferko believed that the C.II marked with black circles was Richthofen's machine (based, apparently, on close scrutiny of the photo and a dubious identification of the officer seated atop that C.II). However, it is more likely that the machine fifth from the right – marked primarily with a black "X" – was actually his aircraft, based on our close examinations of the photo. While there have been a number of recent re-interpretations of the light factory finishes applied to the early Roland C.IIs, we have again opted for a traditional approach. A pale overall finish, possibly sprayed on, is in evidence in many photos and is here presented as a light blue or blue-gray, with white backgrounds for the national insignia. Such a "sky camouflage" was widely employed on many German aircraft contemporary with the early Rolands. It is perhaps worth noting that, in his article in von Eberhardt's *Unsere Luftstreitkräfte* (Berlin, 1930), Eduard von Schleich captioned the photo of his own C.II as "*Auf meiner Maschine (Walfisch). Schutzanstrich: hellblau und Weiss.*"

3. Fokker E.III flown by *Lt.* Manfred von Richthofen, *Kasta* 8 of *Kagohl* 2. There was little to distinguish the E.III crashed by Richthofen from dozens of similar machines, if we are to judge from the available photos. The military serial number, unfortunately, is not visible in any of the available images. Richthofen's E.III is portrayed in the usual beige or pale yellow/tan finish which is the usual interpretation of the appearance of most *Eindecker* machines. This either resulted from the application of clear-doped, unbleached linen or dyed or color-doped fabric. As is so often the case, this *Eindecker* evidenced considerable fabric staining typical of rotary-engined Fokkers from this period. The engine cowling and metal nose panels no doubt displayed the usual 'engine-turned' effect.

4. Albatros D.I 381/16 (or 391/16) flown by *Lt.* Manfred von Richthofen, *Jasta* 2. This profile is based on interpretation of the newly-surfaced photo MvR5, as well as on other *Jasta* 2 Albatros D.Is. The wings and tailplane/elevator left the factory camouflaged in two (or possibly three) terrain camouflage colors. In his article on the Albatros D.I in the French periodical *L'Aerophile* (based on study of the captured 391/16 and 497/16), Jean Lagorgette wrote that, "The wing fabric, like the fuselage plywood, is painted green and brown-red (maroon) on the upper side and pale blue in the lower side, like the Fokker and Roland [D.II] are." There are two small fabric samples from the captured D.I "G.17" in the Imperial War Museum, and these are colored Methuen 3E6, an olive or "sage green," and a brown reported as Methuen 6E8, described as "Rust" or burnt sienna. Thus a dark green and reddish brown were certainly used, perhaps along with a lighter shade of Brunswick Green; those three colors were definitely applied to the first batches of the later Johannisthal-built Albatros D.III machines. The undersides of the wings and tail were painted light sky blue. As noted elsewhere, the plywood-covered fuselage of this machine appears to have been thinly overpainted (or stained) a dark color, most likely some hue which matched brother Lothar's description of "various earth colors." Note that the white sections of the cross insignia were also subdued with an overcoat; Richthofen's later red overpainting of the national emblems demonstrates that this was a favorite practice. The late historian Alex Imrie was of the opinion that many early Albatros D.I and D.II aircraft (particularly those of *Jasta* 2) had their plywood fuselages "stained a lighter reddish-brown, and varnished; random brushed blotches of this stain [were] seen on the fabric rudder." Note the white ring painted around the nose, and an (apparently) white spinner – both features of the later D.II which is assumed to also have been Richthofen's machine.

5. Albatros D.II 481/16 flown by *Lt.* Manfred von Richthofen, *Jasta* 2. This machine was one of the first batch of 50 D.IIs ordered by *Idflieg* in July 1916. Again, it is certain that this machine had its fabric-covered flying surfaces camouflaged in two or (more likely) three colors on upper surfaces: dark olive green, pale Brunswick Green and a reddish-brown, with pale blue undersides. These three colors were in fairly standard use on aircraft from many German manufacturers at this time. For instance, a British report on an OAW-built Albatros C.III (C.2363/17) described the upper surfaces as painted in "...large patches of burnt sienna and light and dark green blending into one another. Undersurfaces very pale blue." As can be seen in the familiar and also the newly-discovered photos of this machine, the plywood fuselage appears to have been overpainted or stained in a manner similar to that seen on the previous D.I. As noted, a white nose ring and white spinner are in evidence on this aircraft.

6. Albatros D.III 2006/16 flown by *Lt.* Manfred von Richthofen, *Jasta* 11. This is the now well-known machine which was reportedly 'handed down' to brother Lothar, and which Lothar described as having "a red band around the fuselage." As related in the text and captions for photos MvR13–15, it can now be determined that this was 2006/16. It also appears to have borne a red spinner, but the rest of the machine seems to have remained in the factory finish. The rudder was covered in clear-doped linen fabric and the wings would have been finished as described above.

7. Albatros D.III *"Le Petit Rouge,"* flown by *Lt.* Manfred von Richthofen, *Jasta* Boelcke and *Jasta* 11. Certainly one of the most famous and iconic aircraft of the war, this machine nonetheless remains enigmatic in a number of ways. As noted in the text, its military serial number is still unknown – though 1991/16 is a likely possibility for the reasons explained. The entire fuselage and all tail surfaces were overpainted a distinctive dark red, and this color was also applied to the wheel covers, undercarriage and all struts as well. The national insignia on the fuselage and vertical tail surfaces were also thinly overpainted in red, but these markings remained slightly discernible; oddly, the Albatros factory logo on the rudder was carefully left uncovered. It is believed that the wings retained their factory finish. As described on another *Jasta*

11 Albatros D.III (Georg Simon's 2015/16, captured in June 1917), the upper wing surfaces were camouflaged in large sections of "a mixture of pale Brunswick Green and white, dark Venetian Red, Olive Green," with the "Undersurfaces of all planes painted sky blue." The reason for Richthofen's choice of red has been the subject for speculation by many writers – some of it quite outlandish. It was certainly an effective way of ensuring that comrades could identify his machine in the air, and it facilitated the recognition of his plane by flak batteries and the *Luftschutz Offiziere* (air defense officers) whose reports helped provide confirmation of his victories. We can do no better than to once again quote the astute observations of Alex Imrie: "This use of red was fostered by *Jagdstaffel* Boelcke, the unit in which Richthofen had served until he was given command of *Jagdstaffel* 11... and caused him to develop a more obvious red as his own color, which he also felt was particularly appropriate for him personally, since red was the regimental color of his old regiment..."

8. Albatros D.III 1996/16 flown by *Oblt.* Manfred von Richthofen, *Jasta* 11. Also well-described in the previous text, this machine is believed to have been Hans-Georg Eduard "Edy" Lübbert's half-blue, half-yellow D.III that was used by Richthofen to achieve his 27th victory on 17 March 1917. Historian Ed Ferko determined that 1996/16 had served as a *Jasta* 11 plane from 21 January until 11 May, before going to *FF(A)* 263. As previously explained there are a few problems with identifying this machine as Lübbert's machine, but it is presented here as one plausible interpretation. It is also likely that the blue and yellow sections were reversed on the starboard side of the fuselage, as evidenced in photo MvR23.

9. Aviatik C.II flown by *Rittm.* Manfred von Richthofen. On 3 May 1917, Richthofen paid a visit to Bad Homburg vor der Höhe to experience the great honor of meeting *Kaiserin* Auguste Victoria and her retinue. He had been flown there in this Aviatik C.II, piloted by his friend Fritz von Falkenhayn. Richthofen subsequently demonstrated a flight for the empress, presumably in this machine. The Aviatik C.II was produced in relatively small numbers and saw limited use; information on the type's camouflage and finishes is consequently lacking. The particular example seen with Richthofen and Falkenhayn displayed an interesting two-tone camouflage applied in soft-edged diagonal stripes on the fuselage. Jim Miller's profile shows one possible interpretation, while other colors such as light olive green and brown are also possible.

124

10. LFG Roland D.III test-flown by *Rittm.* Manfred von Richthofen. This prototype aircraft was test-flown by Richthofen at Adlershof, sometime in the period 16–18 May 1917. A post-war British report on a captured Bulgarian Roland D.III, serial 3007/17, indicated that its color scheme consisted of "...large patches of brown and green blending into one another. Undersurfaces pale blue and white." Additionally, the observant French aviation journalist Jean Lagorgette described the upper surface colors of a captured Roland D.II as *"vert et marron."*

11. Albatros D.V 1177/17 flown by *Rittm.* Manfred von Richthofen. Two photos taken during Richthofen's visit to Gontrode (MvR31–32) in early June 1917 show this D.V flamboyantly painted overall red, including the wings. It would appear that this was D.V 1177/17, which is simply described in the combat reports for victories 54 through 56 as having a "red body." The red paint was thinly applied over the entire national insignia on all surfaces. Though it is possible that the wing undersides remained light blue, it is likely they were red as well. In photos MvR31–32, it can be seen that the factory-applied camouflage sections of olive green and mauve on the top wing were still slightly visible through the red overpaint.

12. Albatros D.V flown by *Rittm.* Manfred von Richthofen, *JG* I, 6 July 1917. This is the famous machine in which Richthofen was wounded on 6 July 1917. The nose and tail were painted red (partially covering the national insignia as usual), as were the wheel covers and all struts. Unusually, the upper surfaces of both wings were also painted deep red, once again almost obliterating the cross emblems. Most of the fuselage seems to have remained in its factory finish of clear-varnished plywood, yet the white border to the fuselage cross presents a very subdued appearance in nearly every photo of this machine. Richthofen's combat report for his victory of 2 July indicates he was flying this D.V that day, for it tersely describes the finish as "hood [engine cowling], tail, decks [wings] red."

13. Albatros D.V flown by *Rittm.* Manfred von Richthofen, *JG* I, 2–6 July 1917. This profile is a provisional depiction of the Albatros D.V used by Richthofen to visit Moorsele during the time between 2 July and 6 July 1917 (photos MvR37–38). It is believed this same machine was later flown by *Lt.* Franz Müller with altered tail colors. It displayed the markings that had apparently only recently been prescribed as the official unit marking for *Jasta* 11. This consisted of the application of 'Richthofen red'

to the entire nose forward of the cockpit, as well as to all struts, the undercarriage and wheel covers. It is likely this machine was primarily assigned to some other *Jasta* 11 pilot at the time, and Richthofen was merely borrowing it (a frequent practice for the *Rittmeister*) during his trip to Moorsele. The area around the fuselage cross was painted over in a dark color thought to have been green, and this extended to the white border of the cross. The green section was bordered by a thin white band at its leading edge. The tail section has been tentatively portrayed as painted red and white. When photographed much later as Müller's primary machine (photo MvR39), the entire tail section had been repainted white. The wings remained in their factory application of dark green and mauve (lilac) camouflage on the top surfaces with light blue undersides.

14. Albatros D.V 2059/17 flown by *Rittm.* Manfred von Richthofen, *JG* I. The well-known photos of *Gen.* Ludendorff's visit to *Jasta* 11 at Markebeke provide the basis for this profile of 2059/17, most likely used by Richthofen to score his 58th and 59th victories. The painting of this D.V seems to have been done in stages. The nose forward of the cockpit was first painted in the deep red *Jasta* 11 unit marking as described above, along with the wheels and struts. Then, apparently later, the rest of the fuselage and tail were overpainted in a slightly thinner (?) red to denote the *Rittmeister's* machine. The 'more intense' red of the nose can just be discerned in first-generation prints of the familiar photos MvR40 and MvR41. The white border to the fuselage cross was painted over, but that around the rudder insignia was carefully left untouched. For once, the military serial number on the fin is quite visible on the photos, and was either left uncovered by the red coat or repainted.

15. Fokker F.I 102/17 flown by *Rittm.* Manfred von Richthofen, *JG* I. For years the colors of this iconic machine have been the subject of almost as much controversy among enthusiasts as those of its sister aircraft, Voss' F.I 103/17. Most readers will be aware of the minor structural differences between the pre-production F.I machines from the Dr.I aircraft: the three F.I aircraft lacked lower wingtip skids and featured slightly smaller wing areas, as well as slightly curved leading edges to their tailplanes. The "streaky camouflaged" fuselage lacked the usual undersurface blue edging on the lower longeron position that is invariably visible on factory-finished Dr.Is, and the camouflage exhibits a paler appearance than that seen on most production triplanes. This initially led to a contention that the three F.Is were first painted entirely light blue then streaked on the upper and side surfaces with the usual Fokker olive camouflage. For what it's worth, around 1961 Alex Imrie interviewed Voss' mechanic Karl Timm, and asked him pointed questions about the finish of 103/17. Imrie stated: "Herr Timm states that this aircraft was colored grey, the forward part of the fuselage and the engine cowling were a very dark grey, to use Timm's words an 'earth grey', while the shade used aft of the cockpit and on the tail unit was 'silver grey'; all undersurfaces were colored light sky blue, and the top surface of the mainplanes were streaked in dark and light areas with various shades of grey." The RFC report on the (admittedly) wrecked remains of 103/17 noted that, "…the entire upper and side surfaces are doped in various shades of green, blue and grey which takes the form of streaks applied at various angles… Lower surfaces are greyish blue." These accounts are quoted here as it is assumed that the factory finishes of 102 and 103/17 were very similar. Many now contend that the upper surfaces of both of these machines were not painted blue before the streaking was applied, but rather were painted in the same manner as the Dr.Is. Jim Miller's superb profile presents a very plausible compromise interpretation of the available evidence. The engine cowling was most likely the factory finish of a solid dark greyish olive. The wheel covers were, however, distinctive in the application of a half-dark, half-pale application of the fuselage colors which merged where they met; this is particularly evident in the motion picture film of this triplane shot by Anthony Fokker.

16. Albatros C.IX flown by *Rittm.* Manfred von Richthofen, *JG* I. One of only three Albatros C.IX aircraft constructed, this machine was used as a personal transport by Richthofen in September and October 1917. The various photos of this unique plane (MvR50–56) show that it was neatly painted entirely red on all surfaces, while carefully leaving the national insignia untouched. Such a flamboyant color scheme would have served as a very potent publicity ploy during visits home, and would have been expected of *der rote Kampfflieger* by the adoring German public. As noted in the text, this machine was also used by Lothar von Richthofen, and was photographed with Werner Voss during a visit to Krefeld. It survived the war and was displayed in the *Deutsche Luftfahrt Sammlung* in Berlin in the 1930s, but was destroyed by Allied bombing in WWII.

17. Fokker Dr.I 114/17 flown by *Rittm.* Manfred von Richthofen. Photo MvR57 shows that this machine displayed the typical Fokker factory streaked olive (greenish-brown) finish on upper surfaces. As on all Fokker Dr.Is, this machine left the Fokker factory with an outdated form of national insignia: the Iron Cross insignia on the upper wings and fuselage were on square white fields and the rudder was painted wholly white as a background for the cross. On the light blue undersides of the lower wings, the crosses were often painted on white backgrounds or sometimes on a panel of natural-doped fabric. This type of insignia had been out of date since 29 October 1916, when 5-cm white borders had been mandated for all crosses on dark surfaces. It was fairly standard practice in *Jasta* 11 to correct the out-of-date insignia by painting out the residue of the white fields to leave only the required 5 cm wide white borders; this had been done on 114/17 by the time photo MvR57 was taken. It is presumed this painting was generally done with a dark solid application of the olive camouflage color, which was even carried out on the rudder. It is just possible that the cowling of this machine had been painted red – which would become part of the standard *Jasta* 11 unit livery – but this is impossible to determine from the photo so we have opted for a conservative interpretation. Interplane struts were probably still in the factory finish of the blue undersurface color.

18. Pfalz Dr.I 3050/17 test-flown by *Rittm.* Manfred von Richthofen. This prototype Pfalz Dr.I was test flown by Richthofen at the Pfalz factory in Speyer sometime between the 13th and 19th of December, 1917. It displayed the typical Pfalz company overall silver finish, so familiar from the Pfalz D.III and D.IIIa. Other than the black national insignia and data stenciling, it carried no other distinguishing markings.

19. Fokker Dr.I 152/17 flown by *Rittm.* Manfred von Richthofen, *JG* I. This familiar Dr.I displays the classic color scheme adopted by Richthofen for most of the triplanes he flew as commander of *JG* I. As noted, his combat reports for victories 64 to 66 describe the finish of this machine as "red upper deck, red cowling, red wheels and red tail." As Alex Imrie was the first to point out, the red tail coloring on 152/17 was extended up the top fuselage decking almost all the way to the cockpit – clearly visible in photo MvR65. In common with other *Jasta* 11 triplanes by this time, all struts were red as well. Again quoting Alex Imrie: "The manner in which his various triplanes were painted – with the top surfaces of the upper wing, engine cowling, and tail unit in red – provided an almost completely red aircraft when viewed from above, which was the position from which identification was required when leading his formation – i.e., as leader he was out in front and lower than the other machines." If this was the machine that was preserved in Berlin's *Zeughaus* Museum and was labeled as Richthofen's machine, it had been painted completely red by that time; however, it remains impossible to verify that the Museum plane was indeed 152/17.

20. Albatros D.V 4479/17 (?) flown by *Rittm.* Manfred von Richthofen, *JG* I. This D.V was flown to the *Jasta* 5 airfield at Boistrancourt by Richthofen on 13 March 1918. It was apparently a former *Jasta* 4 machine, for it displayed the remnants of the black "wound ribbon" marking of that *Staffel* on its fuselage. By this time it was probably a "hack" machine and the spiral ribbon had been overpainted to subdue it, leaving only a portion of the original black ribbon visible on the metal cowling. The nose and tail were painted a dark color, most likely either red or chrome yellow. The wings were covered in five-color printed camouflage fabric. The serial number of this machine has been reported as 4479/17, but that is not confirmed.

21. Fokker Dr.I (*Jasta* 6) flown by *Rittm.* Manfred von Richthofen, *JG* I. On 17 March 1918, Richthofen paid another call on the men of *Jasta* 5 while flying this *Jasta* 6 Fokker Dr.I. Some of the most familiar photos of the *Rittmeister* ever taken were produced on that occasion, and they show that this triplane displayed standard *Jagdstaffel* 6 livery. The tailplane and elevators were vividly striped in black and white, and the cowling was black as well. The rudder was overpainted a dark color to produce the standard 5cm white border to the cross; we have provisionally chosen to portray the rudder as black. In addition, the leading edges of all outer wingtips were painted over in a highly contrasting dark color, probably in an attempt to provide identification from ahead. This color may have been black, red, or yellow. The wheel covers displayed the usual Fokker camouflage application of dark outer rims and lighter centers, and this Dr.I was fitted a rectangular access panel just aft of the cowling in the manner of all *Jasta* 6 triplanes.

22. Fokker Dr.I 161/17 flown by *Rittm.* Manfred von Richthofen, *JG* I. Exactly one month prior to his death, on 21 March 1918, the *JG* I commander visited Boistrancourt yet again – no doubt to coordinate efforts in the 2. *Armee* area on this momentous opening day of Germany's great offensive. At that time he flew Dr.I 161/17. Three photos snapped by Hans-Joachim von Hippel show

that this triplane exhibited the usual finish for one of the *Rittmeister's* triplanes: red engine cowling, upper wing, wheels, struts, and tail section. Once again the red coloring extended forward on the top decking of the fuselage almost to the cockpit.

23. Fokker Dr.I 477/17 flown by *Rittm.* Manfred von Richthofen, *JG* I. Unfortunately, there are no known photos which can be unequivocally proven to show Richthofen's Dr.I 477/17. Ironically, it was by far the most successful of all of his Triplane mounts, for he used it to achieve victories 67 through 70, 72, 73, 75 and 77–78 in March/April 1918 – nine in all. Richthofen's combat reports indicate that it carried his usual color scheme, as illustrated in photos of 127/17, 152/17, and 161/17. This consisted of the red top surface of the upper wing, red tail (again, this presumably was extended forward on the fuselage top decking), red wheels, and red cowling. The latter two markings were also part of the usual *Jasta* 11 color display, and it is very likely that all struts were red as well. Since this was a very important machine, we have decided to include this speculative depiction of it, even without available photos – based on the combat report description and the standard practice seen on the other planes. By the time the *Rittmeister* scored his 77th and 78th victories in 477/17 on 7 April 1918, it is likely that the cross insignia had been changed to the early form of *Balkenkreuz* emblem employed by *JG* I, and the rudder had been repainted white as a background for the new insignia. However, depicting the machine in those markings is even more speculative and has not been attempted here.

24. Fokker Dr.I 127/17 flown by *Rittm.* Manfred von Richthofen, *JG* I. This Dr.I was dispatched from the Fokker factory at Schwerin on 29 October 1917. Richthofen's combat reports for his victories 71, 74, and 76 describe the usual finish for this machine: "red upper deck, red hood, red wheels and red tail." The familiar photo MvR71 (possibly taken at Phalempin airfield in late February 1918, when Richthofen visited *Jasta* 30) records the appearance of this machine before that finish was completed. The white rudder had been painted over with streaky camouflage to produce a 5cm-wide white border to the cross, but the national insignia on wings and fuselage were untouched. At that time the cowling may have been red but no other markings had yet been applied. Photos MvR72 and 73 show it at Léchelle in its final scheme, as portrayed in the color profile. The red overpainting of the white cross field on the port side of the fuselage was either incomplete or had degraded, resulting in a smudged appearance.

25. Fokker Dr.I 425/17 flown by *Rittm*. Manfred von Richthofen, *JG* I, March 1918. The now classic photos (MvR74 and 75) show this legendary machine at Léchelle in its overall dark red color scheme, with pristine Iron Cross national insignia. This aircraft has been the subject of more discussion, argument, and portrayals than any of the rest of Richthofen's machines. Many souvenir portions of it survive in museums and private collections on three continents, and these fabric pieces and structural remnants have been the subject of intense scrutiny. The photos show an extremely uniform appearance of the red paint, and some have suggested that this machine was spray-painted red at *AFP* 2, or at the Fokker factory, prepared specifically for Richthofen. Extant fabric pieces show no evidence of olive camouflage streaking beneath the red paint, though the undersurface blue is present (beneath the red) on pieces from the undersides of the machine. Some of the paint on the port side of the fuselage beneath the cockpit can be seen to have been flaking off in the photos, and no factory olive is evident where the paint has come off. Camouflage and pigment expert Alan Toelle has examined several pieces of fabric from this machine, and determined that the red colorant in the paint was vermilion (mercuric sulphide).

26. Fokker Dr.I 425/17 flown by *Rittm*. Manfred von Richthofen, *JG* I, April 1918. At some point the Iron Crosses were altered to *Balkenkreuz* format following the 17 March directive. The first *Balkenkreuz* emblems were thick crosses of roughly 1:3 ratio (width to length). Later in April, more white paint was employed to alter the black crosses on fuselage and rudder to more closely meet the officially specified ratio of 1:4, resulting in the appearance seen in photo MvR76. A surviving piece of the rudder fabric reveals that the original red rudder fabric was removed and replaced with new fabric that was painted white during the conversion to *Balkenkreuz* format, for there is no evidence of any red paint beneath the white.

Kampfflieger Richthofen † genannt der rote Flieger, mit einem Jagdflugzeug vor einem Erkundigungsflug kurz vor seinem Aufstieg.

Above: The caption to this rare photograph describes it as "Combat pilot Richthofen † called the red flier, with a combat plane shortly before his taking off on a reconnaissance flight." The tail of the Dr.I behind him appears to be a lighter color than red (though light angles could sometimes play tricks with the orthochrome film of the day) so it is not known if it was one of his regular mounts or whether he even flew this particular plane. Still, it is a "new" photo that shows him shortly before his death because the plane bears *Balkenkreuz* insignia. Just over Richthofen's head, the black and white leading edge of the upper wing of *Lt.* Richard Wenzl's Dr.I (seen in other photographs) is visible.

Pour le Mérite Winners by Date of Award

Recipient	Date of Award
Hptm. Oswald Boelcke	January 12, 1916
Oblt. Max Immelmann	January 12, 1916
Oblt. Hans-Joachim Buddecke	April 14, 1916
Lt. Kurt Wintgens	July 1, 1916
Lt. Max *Ritter* von Mulzer	July 8, 1916
Lt. Otto Parschau	July 10, 1916
Lt. Walter Höhndorf	July 20, 1916
Oblt. Ernst *Freiherr* von Althaus	July 21, 1916
Lt. Wilhelm Frankl	August 12, 1916
Hptm. Rudolf Berthold	October 12, 1916
Lt. Gustav Leffers	November 5, 1916
Lt. Albert Dossenbach	November 11, 1916
Oblt. Hans Berr	December 4, 1916
Rittm. Manfred *Freiherr* von Richthofen	January 12, 1917
Genlt. Ernst von Hoeppner	April 8, 1917
Oberst Hermann von der Lieth-Thomsen	April 8, 1917
Lt. Werner Voss	April 8, 1917
Oblt. Fritz Otto Bernert	April 23, 1917
Lt. Karl-Emil Schaefer	April 26, 1917
Oblt. Kurt Wolff	May 4, 1917
Lt. Heinrich Gontermann	May 14, 1917
Lt. Lothar *Freiherr* von Richthofen	May 14, 1917
Lt. Carl Allmenröder	June 14, 1917
Hptm. Ernst Brandenburg	June 14, 1917
Hptm. Paul *Freiherr* von Pechmann	July 31, 1917
Hptm. Adolf *Ritter* von Tutschek	August 3, 1917
Oblt. Eduard *Ritter* von Dostler	August 6, 1917
Fkpt. Peter Strasser	August 30, 1917
Lt. Max *Ritter* von Müller	September 3, 1917
Hptm. Rudolf Kleine	October 4, 1917
Lt. Walter von Bülow-Bothkamp	October 8, 1917
Lt. Curt Wüsthoff	November 22, 1917
Lt. Erwin Böhme	November 24, 1917
Lt. Julius Buckler	December 4, 1917
Lt. Hans Klein	December 4, 1917
Hptm. Eduard *Ritter* von Schleich	December 4, 1917
Hptm. Alfred Keller	December 4, 1917
Kptlt. Friedrich Christiansen	December 11, 1917
Lt. Heinrich Bongartz	December 23, 1917
Oblt. Hermann Fricke	December 23, 1917
Oblt. Hans-Jürgen Horn	December 23, 1917
Hptm. Bruno Loerzer	February 12, 1918
Lt. Heinrich Kroll	March 29, 1918
Kptlt. Horst *Freiherr* Treusch von Buttlar-Brandenfels	April 9, 1918
Oblt. Ernst Udet	April 9, 1918
Lt. Carl Menckhoff	April 23, 1918
Hptm. Hermann Köhl	May 21, 1918
Oblt. Erich Löwenhardt	May 31, 1918
Lt. Fritz Pütter	May 31, 1918
Oblt. Hermann Göring	June 2, 1918
Lt. Friedrich Nielebock	June 2, 1918
Lt. Rudolf Windisch	June 6, 1918
Lt. Wilhelm Paul Schreiber	June 8, 1918
Lt. Hans Kirschstein	June 24, 1918
Oblt. Otto Kissenberth	June 30, 1918
Lt. Emil Thuy	June 30, 1918
Lt. Peter Rieper	July 7, 1918
Lt. Fritz Rumey	July 10, 1918
Lt. Josef Jacobs	July 18, 1918
Lt. zur See Gotthard Sachsenberg	August 5, 1918
Hptm. Franz Walz	August 9, 1918
Lt. Josef Veltjens	August 16, 1918
Lt. Karl Bolle	August 28, 1918
Lt. Theo Osterkamp	September 2, 1918
Oblt. Fritz *Ritter* von Röth	September 8, 1918
Lt. Otto Könnecke	September 26, 1918
Lt. Walter Blume	September 30, 1918
Lt. Wilhelm Griebsch	September 30, 1918
Hptm. Leo Leonhardy	October 2, 1918
Oblt. Robert *Ritter* von Greim	October 8, 1918
Oblt. Jürgen von Grone	October 13, 1918
Oblt. Erich Homburg	October 13, 1918
Oblt. Albert Müller-Kahle	October 13, 1918
Oblt. Oskar *Freiherr* von Boenigk	October 25, 1918
Lt. Franz Büchner	October 25, 1918
Lt. Arthur Laumann	October 25, 1918
Lt. Oliver *Freiherr* von Beaulieu-Marconnay	October 26, 1918
Lt. Karl Thom	November 1, 1918
Lt. Paul Bäumer	November 2, 1918
Lt. Ulrich Neckel	November 8, 1918
Lt. Carl Degelow	November 9, 1918

Pour le Mérite Winners Alphabetically

Recipient	Date of Award	Recipient	Date of Award
Lt. Carl Allmenröder	June 14, 1917	*Hptm.* Rudolf Kleine	October 4, 1917
Oblt. Ernst *Freiherr* von Althaus	July 21, 1916	*Hptm.* Hermann Köhl	May 21, 1918
Lt. Paul Bäumer	November 2, 1918	*Lt.* Otto Könnecke	September 26, 1918
Lt. Oliver *Freiherr* von Beaulieu-Marconnay	October 26, 1918	*Lt.* Heinrich Kroll	March 29, 1918
Oblt. Fritz Otto Bernert	April 23, 1917	*Lt.* Arthur Laumann	October 25, 1918
Oblt. Hans Berr	December 4, 1916	*Lt.* Gustav Leffers	November 5, 1916
Hptm. Rudolf Berthold	October 12, 1916	*Hptm.* Leo Leonhardy	October 2, 1918
Lt. Walter Blume	September 30, 1918	*Oberst* Hermann von der Lieth-Thomsen	April 8, 1917
Lt. Erwin Böhme	November 24, 1917	*Hptm.* Bruno Loerzer	February 12, 1918
Hptm. Oswald Boelcke	January 12, 1916	*Oblt.* Erich Löwenhardt	May 31, 1918
Oblt. Oskar *Freiherr* von Boenigk	October 25, 1918	*Lt.* Carl Menckhoff	April 23, 1918
Lt. Karl Bolle	August 28, 1918	*Lt.* Max *Ritter* von Müller	September 3, 1917
Lt. Heinrich Bongartz	December 23, 1917	*Oblt.* Albert Müller-Kahle	October 13, 1918
Hptm. Ernst Brandenburg	June 14, 1917	*Lt.* Max *Ritter* von Mulzer	July 8, 1916
Lt. Julius Buckler	December 4, 1917	*Lt.* Ulrich Neckel	November 8, 1918
Oblt. Hans-Joachim Buddecke	April 14, 1916	*Lt.* Friedrich Nielebock	June 2, 1918
Lt. Franz Büchner	October 25, 1918	*Lt.* Theo Osterkamp	September 2, 1918
Lt. Walter von Bülow-Bothkamp	October 8, 1917	*Lt.* Otto Parschau	July 10, 1916
Kptlt. Horst *Freiherr* Treusch von Buttlar-Brandenfels	April 9, 1918	*Hptm.* Paul *Freiherr* von Pechmann	July 31, 1917
Kptlt. Friedrich Christiansen	December 11, 1917	*Lt.* Fritz Pütter	May 31, 1918
Lt. Carl Degelow	November 9, 1918	*Lt.* Lothar *Freiherr* von Richthofen	May 14, 1917
Lt. Albert Dossenbach	November 11, 1916	*Rittm.* Manfred *Freiherr* von Richthofen	January 12, 1917
Oblt. Eduard *Ritter* von Dostler	August 6, 1917	*Lt.* Peter Rieper	July 7, 1918
Lt. Wilhelm Frankl	August 12, 1916	*Oblt.* Fritz *Ritter* von Röth	September 8, 1918
Oblt. Hermann Fricke	December 23, 1917	*Lt.* Fritz Rumey	July 10, 1918
Oblt. Hermann Göring	June 2, 1918	*Lt. zur See* Gotthard Sachsenberg	August 5, 1918
Lt. Heinrich Gontermann	May 14, 1917	*Lt.* Karl-Emil Schaefer	April 26, 1917
Oblt. Robert *Ritter* von Greim	October 8, 1918	*Hptm.* Eduard *Ritter* von Schleich	December 4, 1917
Lt. Wilhelm Griebsch	September 30, 1918	*Lt.* Wilhelm Paul Schreiber	June 8, 1918
Oblt. Jürgen von Grone	October 13, 1918	*Fkpt.* Peter Strasser	August 30, 1917
Lt. Walter Höhndorf	July 20, 1916	*Lt.* Karl Thom	November 1, 1918
Genlt. Ernst von Hoeppner	April 8, 1917	*Lt.* Emil Thuy	June 30, 1918
Oblt. Erich Homburg	October 13, 1918	*Hptm.* Adolf *Ritter* von Tutschek	August 3, 1917
Oblt. Hans-Jürgen Horn	December 23, 1917	*Oblt.* Ernst Udet	April 9, 1918
Oblt. Max Immelmann	January 12, 1916	*Lt.* Josef Veltjens	August 16, 1918
Lt. Josef Jacobs	July 18, 1918	*Lt.* Werner Voss	April 8, 1917
Hptm. Alfred Keller	December 4, 1917	*Hptm.* Franz Walz	August 9, 1918
Lt. Hans Kirschstein	June 24, 1918	*Lt.* Rudolf Windisch	June 6, 1918
Oblt. Otto Kissenberth	June 30, 1918	*Lt.* Kurt Wintgens	July 1, 1916
Lt. Hans Klein	December 4, 1917	*Oblt.* Kurt Wolff	May 4, 1917
		Lt. Curt Wüsthoff	November 22, 1917

Index

Adam, Hans: 87
Adams, Alfred T.: 119
Adams, Ronald G.H.: 120
Allmenröder, Carl: 21, 23, 28, 36, 49–50, 63, 69
Allmenröder, Wilhelm: 28
Andrews, Frederick S.: 119
Applin, Richard: 119
Arnim, Sixt von: 34–35
Auer, Hans: 98
Auguste Victoria, *Kaiserin*: 24, 43, 73–74, 123
Bäumer, Paul: 43, 47
Bahr, Erich: 40
Bailey, George C.: 118
Baker, C.G.: 56
Baker, Richard P.: 118
Baldó, Carlos Meyer: 85–86
Baldwin, Cuthbert G.: 118
Barford, Kennth P.: 120
Barnes, William A.: 119
Bates, Allan H.: 119
Batten, W.J.: 119
Bauer, Carl: 69
Beebee, Alfred: 119
Bellerby, Herbert: 118
Bennett, Cyril D.: 118
Bentham, George A.: 118
Berr, Hans: 73
Berthold, Rudolf: 17
Bethge, Hans: 39
Betley, Eric: 120
Bird, Algernon F.: 34, 119
Bitsenko, Anastasia: 38
Bockelmann, Wilhelm: 85–86
Boddien, Hans-Helmuth von: 39
Boddy, James A.V.: 119
Bodenschatz, Karl: 33, 35, 39–40, 50, 87, 115
Böhme, Erwin: 15, 17, 38
Böhme, Gerhard: 38
Boelcke, Oswald: 12–19, 27, 38, 41, 48, 53, 55–56, 116
Boelcke, Wilhelm: 15
Boenigk, Oskar von: 43, 47
Bolle, Karl: 43, 47
Bongartz, Heinrich: 43, 47
Bonner, Percy: 118
Boultbee, Arthur E.: 118
Bowman, Leslie S.: 119
Brauneck, Otto: 22–23, 30, 69
Brichta, Geoffrey J.O.: 118
Brown, A. Roy: 43
Buckler, Julius: 43, 47
Buddecke, Hans-Joachim: 17
Büttner, Karl Heinrich: 56

Burkhard, Prof.Dr.: 27
Byrne, Edward: 118
Cameron, Donald: 120
Cameron, Ian G.: 118
Cantle, Leonard H.: 119
Carganico, Viktor: 14, 27, 77
Carl Eduard, Duke (Saxe-Coburg-Gotha): 35
Clarke, Thomas H.: 118
Clarkson, Albert: 118
Clutterbuck, Leonard C.F.: 119
Collishaw, Raymond: 50
Croft, Herbert A.: 118
Crosbee, James B.E.: 118
Cunnell, Douglas C.: 30
Cunniffe, James A.: 119
Cuzner, Alber E.: 119
D'Arcy, Lionel G.: 118
Davies, David E.: 119
de La Tour, Mathieu Tenant: 14
Degelow, Carl: 43, 47
Denovan, Allan M.: 120
Derwin, Edward C.E.: 119
Deullin, Albert: 14
Döring, Kurt von: 35
Doughty, George: 118
Dunn, Reuel: 118
Esser, Karl: 22–23, 69
Everbusch, Alfred: 98
Everbusch, Ernst: 98
Everingham, Guy: 119
Falkenhausen, Ludwig von: 21
Falkenhayn, Fritz von: 73–74, 98, 123
Farquhar, Robert W.: 119
Fenwick, William C.: 118
Ferdinand, Czar (Bulgaria): 27
Festner, Sebastian: 21–22, 49, 69
Fisher, Arthur J.: 118
Flashar, Richard: 41, 104–05
Fletcher, William F.: 119
Fokker, Anthony: 34–35, 38, 86–87, 92, 99–100, 125
Follit, Reginald W.: 119
Frankl, Wilhelm: 17
Franklin, Waldemar: 119
Friedrich, Prince (Prussia): 26
Friedrich Karl, Prince (Prussia): 26
Friedrich Sigismund, Prince (Prussia): 26, 43
Gallie, Albert V.: 120
George, Herbert D.K.: 119
Gerlich, Martin: 79
Gerstenberg, Alfred: 7, 15, 53–54, 77
Gilbert, Christopher G.: 118
Glogau, Emile August: 18

Gontermann, Heinrich: 36
Gosset-Bibby, Gerald M.: 118
Grafe, Winand: 17
Green, Herbert J.: 118
Greig, Oscar: 118
Groos, Gisbert-Wilhelm: 85–86
Gürke, Wilhelm: 41, 103
Gussmann, Siegfried: 39
Haehnelt, Wilhelm: 41
Hall, Gilbert S.: 118
Hallerstein, Hans Haller von: 10
Hampton, George W.B.: 118
Hans Heinrich XI, Prince (Pless): 27
Harding, George H.: 120
Hartmann, *Lt.* von: 22–23
Hawker, Lanoe G.: 18–19, 49, 118
Hay, John: 118
Heagerty, John S.: 119
Heath, Elmer E.: 119
Hesketh, J.E.B.: 119
Hindenburg, Paul von: 23, 25, 27, 43
Hinsch, Hans: 69
Hippel, Hans-Joachim von: 41, 105, 126
Höhndorf, Walter: 17
Höhne, Otto: 17, 57
Hoeppner, Ernst von: 22, 25, 31, 35, 43
Hohberg, *Lt.*: 71
Holck, Count Erich von: 10, 13
Hoppe, Paul: 73
Howlett, Ernest A.: 118
Hunt, Benedict P.G.: 118
Imelmann, Hans: 17–18, 58–59
Immelmann, Max: 14–15, 18, 55
Ivamy, William G.: 120
Jackson, H.M.: 119
Jacobs, Josef: 38, 47, 50
Janzen, Johann: 39
Jones, Erbest D.: 120
Just, Erich: 39
Karjus, Walther: 42–43
Kastner-Kirdorf, Gustav: 15
Keller, Alfred: 16, 43, 47
Kember, Walter: 119
Keyserlingk, Doris Katherina Margarete von: 93, 95
King, Frederick: 118
Kirkham, Frederick J.: 119
Kirmaier, Stefan: 17, 58–59
Klein, Hans: 38, 43, 47
Kleine, Rudolf: 79
Knight, Arthur G.: 118
Köhl, Hermann: 43, 47
Könitz, *Frhr.* von: 10
Könnecke, Otto: 43, 47
Kraske, Prof.Dr.: 31, 50
Krefft, Constantin: 22, 24, 28, 39, 49, 69, 98

Lansdale, Ernest C.: 118
Laumann, Arthur: 43, 47
Lechler, Arthur N.: 119
Lees, James C.: 118
Leggat, Matthew: 120
Lehmann, Wilhelm: 105
Leonhardy, Leo: 43, 47
Leopold, Prince (Bavaria): 38
Lewis, David G.: 120
Lidsey, William J.: 118
Linsingen, Hans-Karl von: 39
Lischke, Kurt: 43
Loerzer, Bruno: 38, 43, 47
Loewenhardt, Erich: 38, 42–43
Lossberg, Friedrich Karl von: 87
Ludendorff, Erich: 23, 27, 79, 85–86, 124
Lübbert, Friedrich Wilhelm: 115
Lübbert, Hans-Georg Eduard: 63–64, 71, 73, 114, 123
Lyncker, Bodo von: 18
MacGregor, Donald A.D.I.: 119
MacKenzie, Keith I.: 119
MacLennan, John E.: 118
Madge, John B.C.: 119
Mai, Josef: 43, 47
May, Wilfrid R.: 43
McCone, John P.: 120
McDonald, Donald P.: 118
McNaughton, Norman G.: 119
McRae, Duncan J.: 118
Mearns, Angus H.: 119
Meyer, Willy: 98
Michaelis, Georg: 34–35, 86–87
Mohnicke, Eberhardt: 9, 33, 35, 85–86, 92
Morris, Lionel B.F.: 17, 48, 118
Mühlig-Hoffmann, Albert: 98
Müller, Franz: 81, 82, 84–85, 124
Müller, Max (*Ritter* von): 17
Murray, Percival W.: 118
Newton, M.E.: 119
Newton, Robert F.: 120
Niederhoff, Alfred: 30
O'Beirne, John I.M.: 118
Osten, Hans-Georg von der: 39, 50, 76, 85–86, 115, 134
Osterkamp, Theo: 47, 50
Osterroht, Paul Henning von: 11, 13, 52–53, 67
Parker, C.A.: 119
Pascoe, Alphonso: 119
Pascoe, Frank G.B.: 119
Pastor, Günther: 36
Paustian, Sebastian: 50
Pearson, Arthur J.: 118
Pierson, H: 119
Plüschow, Wolfgang: 23
Powell, Patrick J.G.: 118
Power-Clutterbuck, James E.: 119

Prance, John E.: 118
Quicke, Sidney H.: 118
Rathbone, George H: 119
Raymond-Barker, Richard: 120
Reading, Vernon J.: 120
Rees, Tom: 17, 48–49, 118
Reibnitz, Nicol von: 50
Reid, Alexander W.: 118
Reimann, Hans: 14–15, 17, 55
Reimann, Leopold: 17
Reinhard, Wilhelm: 33, 85–86
Reusing, Fritz: 12, 38
Richthofen, Albrecht von: 6, 23–24, 30, 32, 35, 38,
    46, 48, 50
Richthofen, Elisabeth von: 6–7, 13, 26, 43, 46, 49
Richthofen, Karl Bolko von: 6, 8, 13, 35, 43, 46, 49
Richthofen, Kunigunde von: 6–7, 9, 13, 19–20, 23,
    26–27, 35, 40, 42–43, 46, 48–50, 76, 92, 114–15
Richthofen, Lothar von: 6, 8, 13, 20–24, 26–28, 30,
    32, 35–36, 38–39, 41, 43, 46, 49–50, 56, 59, 64–65,
    69, 77, 92, 95–96, 103, 122–23, 125
Richthofen, Manfred von: 6–127, 135–36
Richthofen, Wolfram von: 42–43
Russell, William O.: 119
Sachsenberg, Gotthard: 47, 50
Saltzmann, Erich von: 29
Sandel, Jürgen: 18, 57, 61
Schaefer, Karl-Emil: 21–23, 27, 29, 36, 49, 64–66, 69,
    71, 114
Scheffer, Guido: 31, 39
Schlegel, Ernst: 97
Schloemer, Hans: 105
Schoenebeck, Karl-August von: 39, 85–86
Scholtz, Edgar: 43
Sharpe, Thomas S.: 120
Siegert, Wilhelm: 64
Simon, Georg: 22, 69, 123
Smart, Edward T.: 120
Smart, George O.: 119
Smith, Sydney P.: 120
Smyth, James: 118
Sorg, Maximilian: 22
Sparks, Henry J.: 119
Stapenhorst, Eberhard: 85–86
Stead, George: 119
Steinhäuser, Werner: 39, 43
Stewart, Donald J.: 119
Stuart, James M.: 119
Taylor, Joseph B.: 120
Thompson, John: 118
Thomsen, Hermann: 15, 25
Timm, Karl: 125
Todd, Allan S.: 118
Tollervey, Amos G.: 119
Tutschek, Adolf *Ritter* von: 38, 98

Veltjens, Josef: 43, 47
Voss, Max Sr.: 29
Voss, Werner: 21, 27, 29, 31, 34–36, 124–25
Walz, Franz: 43, 47
Warren, Algernon P.: 118
Watt, George M.: 118
Weiss, Hans: 42–43
Welch, Eric A.: 119
Wenzl, Richard: 41–43, 50
Whatley, Hubert A.: 119
Whiteside, Reginald C.: 118
Wilberg, Helmuth: 85–86
Wilhelm II, Kaiser: 19, 23–24, 27, 41
Williams, Coningsby P.: 119
Williams, William H.T.: 119
Wintgens, Kurt: 17
Wolff, Hans-Joachim: 39, 41–43
Wolff, Kurt: 21–24, 28, 35–36, 49–50, 63, 69, 86,
    90–91
Wood, Maurice H.: 119
Woodbridge, Albert E.: 28
Wortmann, Hans: 59, 61–62
Wüsthoff, Curt: 43, 47
Zettemeyer, *Oblt.*: 41
Zeumer, Georg: 10–11, 13–14, 52–53, 114, 122

Aviation Units
Armee-Flug-Park (AFP) 1: 15–16, 56
Armee-Flug-Park (AFP) 2: 127
Brieftauben-Abteilung Metz (B.A.M.): 12–13
Brieftauben-Abteilung Ostende (B.A.O.): 10–13, 52,
    116, 122
Escadrille (Esc.) N3: 14
Escadrille (Esc.) N57: 14
Flieger-Abteilung-Arteilerie (FF(A)) 263: 71–72, 123
Feldflieger-Abteilung (FFA) 69: 10, 52, 116–17
Flieger-Ersatz-Abteilung (FEA) 2: 13, 53, 116
Flieger-Ersatz-Abteilung (FEA) 5: 92
Flieger-Ersatz-Abteilung (FEA) 6: 10, 39, 52, 116
Flieger-Ersatz-Abteilung (FEA) 7: 9, 52, 116
Flieger-Ersatz-Abteilung (FEA) 11: 77
Jagdgeschwader (JG) 1: 16, 28, 31, 33–36, 38–39, 41,
    46, 79, 82, 85, 87, 97–98, 103, 109, 116, 125, 127
Jagdgeschwader (JG) 2: 38, 98
Jagdgeschwader (JG) 3: 38
Jagdstaffel (Jasta) 2/ Boelcke: 15–18, 21, 27, 38, 48,
    56–63, 116, 122–23
Jagdstaffel (Jasta) 4: 17, 28, 38, 42, 102–04, 126
Jagdstaffel (Jasta) 5: 41, 102–07, 126
Jagdstaffel (Jasta) 6: 28, 38, 87, 104–05, 126
Jagdstaffel (Jasta) 7: 28, 38
Jagdstaffel (Jasta) 10: 28, 31, 38
Jagdstaffel (Jasta) 11: 9, 11, 19–24, 28, 31, 34–35, 38,
    40–42, 49, 62–64, 67–68, 71–72, 78, 80, 82, 84–86,
    103, 114–16, 123–25

Jagdstaffel (Jasta) 12: 11, 38, 98

Jagdstaffel (Jasta) 26: 28, 38

Jagdstaffel (Jasta) 28: 27

Jagdstaffel (Jasta) 30: 39

Jagdstaffel (Jasta) 32: 98

Kampfeinsitzer-Kommando (KEK) Jametz: 14

Kampfgeschwader der Obersten Heeresleitung (Kagohl or KG) Nr.2: 13–15, 53, 116, 122

Kampfgeschwader der Obersten Heeresleitung (Kagohl or KG) Nr.3: 79

Kampfstaffel (Kasta) 8: 13–15, 27, 53–54, 116, 122

Kampfstaffel (Kasta) 10: 15

RAF No.3 Squadron: 120

RAF No.46 Squadron: 120

RAF No.52 Squadron: 120

RAF No.73 Squadron: 120

RAF No.209 Squadron: 43–44, 51

RFC No.1 Squadron: 120

RFC No.2 Squadron: 62, 118, 120

RFC No.3 Squadron: 120

RFC No.6 Squadron: 119

RFC No.11 Squadron: 17, 118–19

RFC No.12 Squadron: 17, 118–19

RFC No.13 Squadron: 118–19

RFC No.15 Squadron: 118, 120

RFC No.16 Squadron: 63, 118–19

RFC No.18 Squadron: 118–19

RFC No.19 Squadron: 118–19

RFC No.20 Squadron: 28

RFC No.21 Squadron: 118

RFC No.23 Squadron: 119

RFC No.24 Squadron: 18, 118

RFC No.25 Squadron: 118–19

RFC No.27 Squadron: 118

RFC No.29 Squadron: 118–19

RFC No.32 Squadron: 118

RFC No.40 Squadron: 118

RFC No.41 Squadron: 119–20

RFC No.43 Squadron: 118–19

RFC No.46 Squadron: 34, 119

RFC No.48 Squadron: 119

RFC No.53 Squadron: 119

RFC No.54 Squadron: 120

RFC No.57 Squadron: 119

RFC No.59 Squadron: 119

RFC No.60 Squadron: 119

RFC No.62 Squadron: 119

RFC No.64 Squadron: 119

RFC No.73 Squadron: 119–20

RFC No.79 Squadron: 120

RFC No.82 Squadron: 120

RNAS No.8 Squadron: 118–19

Bibliography

Books

Bodenschatz, Karl. *Jagd in Flanderns Himmel* (Munich: Verlag Knorr & Hirth, 1935)

Bodenschatz, Karl. *Hunting with Richthofen*, trans. by Jan Hayzlett (London: Grub Street, 1996)

Bronnenkant, Lance. *The Blue Max Airmen*, Volume 1 (Aeronaut Books, 2012)

Bronnenkant, Lance. *The Imperial German Eagles in World War I – Their Postcards and Pictures*, Volume 1 (Atglen: Schiffer Publishing, 2006)

Bronnenkant, Lance. *The Imperial German Eagles in World War I – Their Postcards and Pictures*, Volume 2 (Atglen: Schiffer Publishing, 2008)

Bronnenkant, Lance. *The Imperial German Eagles in World War I – Their Postcards and Pictures*, Volume 3(Atglen: Schiffer Publishing, 2011)

Cole, Christopher. *Royal Flying Corps 1915–1916* (London: William Kimber & Co., 1969)

Ferko, A.E. *Richthofen* (Berkhamsted: Albatros Publications, 1995)

Franks, Norman. *Jasta Boelcke* (London: Grub Street, 2004)

Franks, Norman, Frank Bailey, and Rick Duiven. *The Jasta War Chronology* (London: Grub Street, 1998)

Franks, Norman, Frank Bailey, and Russell Guest. *Above the Lines* (London: Grub Street, 1993)

Franks, Norman, Hal Giblin, and Nigel McCrery. *Under The Guns of The Red Baron* (London: Grub Street, 2007)

Gibbons, Floyd. *The Red Knight of Germany* (New York: Bantam Books, 1964)

Grosz, Peter. *Albatros D.III* (Berkhamsted: Albatros Publications, 2003)

Henshaw, Trevor. *The Sky Their Battlefield* (London: Grub Street, 1995)

Herris, Jack. *Germany's Fight Competitions of 1918* (Aeronaut Books: 2013)

Herris, Jack. *Pfalz Aircraft of World War I* (Boulder: Flying Machines Press, 2001)

Imrie, Alex. *The Fokker Triplane* (London: Arms & Armour Press, 1993)

Kilduff, Peter. *Richthofen: Beyond the Legend of the Red Baron* (New York: John Wiley & Sons, 1993)

Kilduff, Peter. *The Red Baron Combat Wing* (London: Arms & Armour Press, 1997)

Kilduff, Peter. *The Illustrated Red Baron* (London: Cassell Group, 1999)

Miller, James F. *Manfred von Richthofen: The Aircraft, Myths and Accomplishments of 'The*

Red Baron' (Crowborough: Chevron Publishing, 2009) O'Connor, Neal. *Aviation Awards of Imperial Germany in World War I and the Men Who Earned Them*, Volume 5 (Stratford: Flying Machines Press, 1998)

Richthofen, Kunigunde von. *Mein Kriegstagebuch* (Berlin: Verlag Ullstein, 1937)

Richthofen, Kunigunde von. *Mother of Eagles: The War Diary of Baroness von Richthofen*, trans. by Suzanne Hayes Fischer (Atglen: Schiffer Publishing, 2001)

Richthofen, Manfred von. *Der rote Kampfflieger* (Berlin: Verlag Ullstein, 1917)

Richthofen, Manfred von. *Der rote Kampfflieger* (Berlin: Verlag Ullstein, 1933)

Richthofen, Manfred von. *Ein Heldenleben* (Berlin: Verllag Ullstein, 1920)

Richthofen, Manfred von. *The Red Baron*, trans. by Peter Kilduff (Garden City: Doubleday, 1969)

Supf, Peter. *Das Buch der deutschen Fluggeschichte*, Volume 2 (Stuttgart: Drei Brunnen Verlag, 1958)

VanWyngarden, Greg. *'Richthofen's Circus': Jagdgeschwader Nr 1* (Botley: Osprey Publllishing, 2004)

VanWyngarden, Greg. *von Richthofen's Flying Circus: Colors and Markings of Jagdgeschwader Nr. 1* (Berkhamsted: Albatros Publications, 1995)

Wenzl, Richard. *Richthofen–Flieger* (Karlsruhe: Badische Zeitung, 1918)

Werner, Prof. Dr. Johannes. *Briefe eines deutschen Kampffliegers an ein junges Mädchen* (Leipzig: Verlag von K.F. Koehler, 1930)

Weyl , A.R. *Fokker: The Creative Years* (London: Aero Publishers, 1965)

Periodicals & Newspapers

Cross & Cockade (Society of WWI Aero Historians) 1969, 1974.
    10:2 "Von Richthofen: A Photo Album Essay," pp.97–152
    15:3 "With Jagdstaffeln 11 and 4" by Georg von der Osten, pp.219–26

Over The Front (League of WWI Aviation Historians) 2004.
    19:1 "Nachrichtenblatt No.18" trans. by Peter Kilduff and Jan Hayzlett, pp.88–91.

Glossary

Armee–Flug–Park (AFP)	Army aviation supply depot
Bericht der Oberste Heeresleitung	(see *Heeresbericht*)
Brieftauben–Abteilung	"Carrier pigeon" unit
CO	Commanding officer
Eindecker	Monoplane
Escadrille (Esc.)	Aviation unit
Fähnenjunker	Junior Officer Candidate
Feldflieger–Abteilung (FFA)	Field aviation unit
Feldflugchef	Chief of Army Field Aviation
Flieger–Abteilung (FA)	Aviation unit
Flieger–Abteilung Artillerie (FA(A))	Artillery cooperation aviation unit
Flieger–Ersatz–Abteilung (FEA)	Aviation replacement unit
Fliegertruppe	Air Service
Fokkerstaffel	Unit equipped with *Eindecker* aircraft
Freiherr	"free lord" title of nobility
FSLt.	naval Flight Sub–Lieutenant
General (Gen.)	General
General der Infanterie	General of the Infantry
Generalfeldmarschall	Field Marshal
Generalleutnant (GenLt.)	Lieutenant General (U.S. Major General)
Generaloberst	Colonel General (U.S. Four–Star General)
Geschwader	Squadron
Geschwaderführer	CO of a *Geschwader*
Grosskampfflugzeug	Large combat plane
Hauptmann (Hptm.)	Captain
Heeresbericht	Army reports
Inspektion der Fliegertruppe (Idflieg)	Inspectorate of Army Air Service
Jagdgeschwader (JG)	Squadron consisting of several *Jagdstaffeln*

Jagdstaffel (Jasta)	Fighter unit
Jastaschule	Fighter pilot training school
Kaiserin	Empress
Kampfeinsitzer–Abteilung	Single–seat fighter unit
Kampfeinsitzer–Kommando (KEK)	Single–seat fighter unit
Kampfeinsitzerstaffel	Single–seat fighter unit
Kampfflieger	Combat aviator
Kampfstaffel (Kasta)	Combat unit
Kampfgeschwader (Kagohl/KG)	Fighting squadron
Kogenluft	Commanding General of the Army Air Service or his staff
Kommandeur der Flieger (Kofl.)	Officer/staff in charge of aviation for an army
Kriegsschule	War school
Kriegstagebuch	War diary
Leutnant (Lt.) – German	2nd Lieutenant
Lieutenant (Lt.) – French	1st Lieutenant
Luftstreitkräfte	Air force
Major	Major
Oberleutnant (Oblt.)	1st Lieutenant
Offizier–Stellvertreter (Offz–Stv.)	Warrant Officer
Ordenskissen	Funeral pillow displaying deceased's decorations
RAF	Royal Air Force
Reichskanzler	Chancellor of Germany
RFC	Royal Flying Corps
Ritter	Knight (honorary title)
Rittmeister (Rittm.)	Cavalry Captain
SLt.	Naval Sub–Lieutenant
Soldat	Private
Stabsoffizier der Flieger (Stofl.)	Aviation officer/staff for an army
Staffel	Unit
Staffelführer	Commanding officer of a *Staffel*
Unteroffizier (Uffz.)	Corporal
Vizefeldwebel (Vzfw.)	Vice Sergeant or Vice Sergeant Major
Werknummer	Factory works number

Errata & Addenda

Volume 3

It turns out that the photo seen on page 27 of Volume 3 is not of Otto Parschau's first victory. We know this thanks to German historians Rainer Absmeier and Reinhard Zankl, who have access to Robert Greim's *Flugbuch*. It includes the same photo and another of the scene, both labeled "*Abschuss am 10.10.15*" ("shot down on 10 October 1915"). Greim's first victim, a Farman from *Escadrille* MF63, manned by *Sgt.* Henri Mahieu and *Sous–Lt.* Henri Merillon, fell that day near Hattonchâtel; so it seems highly likely that the photos were of his victory.

Right: A lithograph portrait of Richthofen.

Above: Artist Arnold Busch created this drawing of Richthofen during a visit in July 1917.

Made in the USA
Monee, IL
25 April 2022

95366809R00083